UNIVERSITY OF ST. THOMAS LIBRARIES

A WORKING NATION

A WORKING NATION
WORKERS, WORK, AND GOVERNMENT IN THE NEW ECONOMY

DAVID T. ELLWOOD, REBECCA M. BLANK,
JOSEPH BLASI, DOUGLAS KRUSE,
WILLIAM A. NISKANEN,
AND KAREN LYNN-DYSON

Russell Sage Foundation • New York

The Russell Sage Foundation

The Russell Sage Foundation, one of the oldest of America's general purpose foundations, was established in 1907 by Mrs. Margaret Olivia Sage for "the improvement of social and living conditions in the United States." The Foundation seeks to fulfill this mandate by fostering the development and dissemination of knowledge about the country's political, social, and economic problems. While the Foundation endeavors to assure the accuracy and objectivity of each book it publishes, the conclusions and interpretations in Russell Sage Foundation publications are those of the authors and not of the Foundation, its Trustees, or its staff. Publication by Russell Sage, therefore, does not imply Foundation endorsement.

BOARD OF TRUSTEES
Ira Katznelson, Chair

Alan S. Blinder	Jennifer L. Hochschild	Eugene Smolensky
Christine K. Cassel	Timothy A. Hultquist	Marta Tienda
Thomas D. Cook	Ellen Condliffe Langemann	Eric Wanner
Robert E. Denham	Cora B. Marrett	
Phoebe C. Ellsworth	Neil J. Smelser	

Library of Congress Cataloging-in-Publication Data

A working nation : workers, work, and government in the new economy / David T. Ellwood . . . [et al.].
  p. cm.
Includes bibliographical references and index.
ISBN 0-87154-264-3 (hardbound)   ISBN 0-87154-247-1 (paperback)
  1. Labor—United States. 2. Industrial relations—United States. 3. Labor policy—United States. I. Ellwood, David T. II. Lynn-Dyson, Karen.

HD8072.5 .W675 2000
331'.0973—dc21   00-036620

Copyright © 2000 by Russell Sage Foundation. All rights reserved. Printed in the United States of America. No part of this publication may be reproduced, stored in a retrieval system, or transmitted in any form or by any means, electronic, mechanical, photocopying, recording, or otherwise, without the prior written permission of the publisher.

Reproduction by the United States Government in whole or in part is permitted for any purpose.

The paper used in this publication meets the minimum requirements of American National Standard for Information Sciences—Permanence of Paper for Printed Library Materials. ANSI Z39.48-1992.

Support for this volume was provided by the Rockefeller Foundation and the Russell Sage Foundation.

RUSSELL SAGE FOUNDATION
112 East 64th Street, New York, New York 10021
10 9 8 7 6 5 4 3 2 1

Contents

ABOUT THE AUTHORS		vii
INTRODUCTION	David T. Ellwood	ix
CHAPTER 1	Winners and Losers in America: Taking the Measure of the New Economic Realities *David T. Ellwood*	1
CHAPTER 2	The New Employee-Employer Relationship *Douglas Kruse and Joseph Blasi*	42
CHAPTER 3	Creating Good Jobs and Good Wages *William A. Niskanen*	92
CHAPTER 4	Enhancing the Opportunities, Skills, and Security of American Workers *Rebecca M. Blank*	105
NOTES		124
REFERENCES		134
INDEX		143

About the Authors

David T. Ellwood is Lucius N. Littauer Professor of Political Economy at the John F. Kennedy School of Government, Harvard University. He is also director of the Aspen Domestic Strategy Group.

Rebecca M. Blank was a member of the Council of Economic Advisers under President Clinton. She is Henry Carter Adams Collegiate Professor of Public Policy, dean of the Gerald R. Ford School of Public Policy, and professor of economics at the University of Michigan.

Joseph Blasi is professor of sociology at the School of Management and Labor Relations, Rutgers University.

Douglas Kruse is professor of economics at the School of Management and Labor Relations, Rutgers University. He is also research associate of the National Bureau of Economic Research.

William A. Niskanen was a member of the Council of Economic Advisers under President Reagan and is chairman of the Cato Institute.

Karen Lynn-Dyson is associate director of the Aspen Institute's Domestic Strategy Group.

Introduction

Work in the U.S. economy is changing in profound ways, creating new opportunities and new inequalities. There are winners and losers, new forms of competition, new pressures, and new calls for action. Yet in the increasingly fractious and partisan atmosphere that has engulfed the nation in recent years, the hope of finding some common understanding about what is happening, much less reaching any sort of consensus on actions (or inaction) that the nation might consider, seems increasingly forlorn. Ignoring the new economic realities could lead to a weaker economy in the future, an increasingly divided society, more uneven opportunities for our children, and potentially even the emergence of demagogues who will exploit the politics of blame and polarization.

The Domestic Strategy Group and Confusion About the Economy

The Aspen Institute's Domestic Strategy Group (DSG) was formed to find common ground. An eminent group of leaders from business, government, labor, local communities, the press, and academia have come together in a multiyear effort to examine the future of work. The group seeks to answer several critical questions: What is happening to work and workers, and what does the future hold? What challenges and opportunities do the economic changes create for firms, workers, families, and communities? And what can we do to meet these challenges?

The group began this effort in the summer of 1997. Experts on technology, trade, workers, the economy, and many other domains came before the group. Their reports, summarized by David Bollier (1998), were fascinating and frustrating. Some argued that the nation was on the verge of a great renaissance, led by technology, that would sweep the nation forward and ultimately produce a vastly more prosperous nation. They pointed to firms engaged in bold and exciting innovations to meet the new challenges. Yet others complained that the nation was mired in a period of limited growth with very modest increases in productivity. Still others pointed to dramatic changes in the distribution of wages and bemoaned the increasing inequality among our workers. All of the presenters had facts and figures aplenty to support their sometimes hyperbolic claims.

Predictably, the group was concerned. How could these thoughtful people reach such different conclusions? Perhaps the problem lay in the data—surely it could not be the case that national income per capita had risen rapidly, while the median earnings of the typical male worker had been flat or falling. Perhaps the confusion involved the short-term struggles of a few during a transition to a new economy. Or in the words of Alan Blinder speaking to the group in August 1997 in Aspen, perhaps the "Goldilocks economy" was really the "Little Girl with the Little Curl: When she was good, she was very, very good, but when she was bad, she was *horrid.*"

The policy conclusions were equally frustrating. Should we do nothing and let the miracle of the new economy unfold? Should we look for ways to intervene and sharply change the structure of work and pay? Or should the government seek to ameliorate the insecurities caused by the changing economic climate and to improve the productivity of workers without intervening in markets per se?

For its meeting the next summer, the group commissioned a series of papers designed to learn about the facts and the directions that the nation should consider for policy. Those papers constitute the chapters in this volume. Each chapter focuses on one of three main issues:

1. How has the changing economy affected the pay of workers and the incomes of families? Who has gained and who has lost as a result of the changing patterns of work and pay in the past quarter century? David Ellwood focuses on these questions in chapter 1.

2. How has the nature of work and the relationship between employees and employers changed in recent years? How much promise is there in so called "high-performance workplace" practices and employee participation in ownership and profits? Douglas Kruse and Joseph Blasi focus on these issues in chapter 2.

3. What should government do about these changes? William Niskanen and Rebecca Blank—former members of the President's Council of Economic Advisers under Ronald Reagan and Bill Clinton, respectively—offer different perspectives on policy in chapters 3 and 4.

Introduction   xi

In effect, then, this volume views the changing economic landscape and potential policy responses through several different lenses: the worker, the relationship between workers and employers, and government policy.

These chapters paint a surprisingly consistent picture both about what is happening and what the nation ought to consider. And they had a powerful effect on the group when they were presented. By the end of the group's meeting in the summer of 1998, DSG members largely concluded that the differences in interpretation were primarily the result not of numbers problems, but rather of the selective reporting or interpretation of facts. Dramatic changes are indeed occurring, and these changes have created both winners and losers, with profound implications for families and children. Industry is changing, but not nearly as fast as some expected or as some believed necessary. And the group charted a direction in the search for ways to meet the challenges and opportunities that the changing economic picture offered. It is our hope that this volume can provide the sort of clarity needed for the nation to understand the challenges we face. We summarize these insights briefly here.

How Has the Changing Economy Affected Workers and Families?

Chapter 1 directly confronts one of the apparent contradictions in economic data: how could per capita national income have risen steadily, while the wages of most male workers stagnated? Where did the money go? Ellwood finds that essentially none of the growth in the economy between 1973 and 1996 went to middle- and working-class male workers—workers with wages in the bottom two-thirds of the distribution. Nearly half of the new income in the economy was paid to women. Indeed one of the most profound changes in the current economy is the increase in work by women and the rise in their wages relative to those of men. This does not mean that women earn as much as men—they do not—only that they have been catching up. Too often discussions of the economy ignore the role of greater work and higher pay for women. Another quarter of wages went to upper-income male workers. And the remainder went to profits. However, profits as a *share* of total national income did not change a great deal, rather capital got the same portion of a larger pie.

Chapter 1 illustrates that the economic fortunes of the nation seem to be shared less uniformly than in previous eras. The 1960s were a period of shared prosperity in which a rising tide really did seem to lift all boats. The 1970s were a time of shared stagnation. And the 1980s and 1990s were a period of divergence, with large winners and losers. Even among women, those at the top did far better during the 1980s and 1990s than those at the middle and bottom.

One might hope that declines for men were offset by increases in earnings for women, and thus families and children were sharing the prosperity even if individuals were not. Unfortunately, the divergence in the fortunes of children was even greater than the divergence in the earnings of individuals. The chapter points to two reasons. First, higher-income women (whose earnings grew the most among women) tend to marry higher-income men (who were the only group of men to experience large earnings gains), thus exacerbating the trends for either group alone. Second, the sharp increase in the number of children in lone-parent families pushed down the economic fortunes of many children who had income from one or fewer earners. Thus children in the top third are vastly better off economically now than they were two decades ago. Children in the bottom are far worse off.

How Has the Relationship Between Workers and Employers Changed and What Might Be Done to Improve It?

In chapter 2 Douglas Kruse and Joseph Blasi suggest that by many measures the connection between workers and employers has weakened, although perhaps not as dramatically as some suggest. The authors report that the risk of displacement and layoff grew in the 1990s, particularly for white-collar workers. Displacement always rises in recessions and falls when the economy is strong. Yet displacement in 1996, which was a good year by almost any measure, was nearly as high as it was during the peak of the 1982 recession. They find an accompanying decline in the fraction of workers with long-term employment with a single firm. And there appears to be a rise in the number of contingent workers. Still the chapter also provides an antidote to the often-exaggerated claims that stable employment connections barely exist anymore, for there remains a considerable number of long-tenure workers, and contingent work has declined in the recent strong economy. Nonetheless, the number has fallen considerably for men.

Kruse and Blasi then examine the impact and prevalence of a variety of what might be labeled "high-performance workplace strategies"— from quality circles to training to self-managed work teams. There is evidence that such practices can improve productivity, but typically only if used in combination. And although they find that a large fraction of firms practice some form of high-performance strategy, few (less than 10 percent) embrace the combination of actions that seems to offer the greatest potential for productivity gains.

Next the authors look at the question of whether so-called shared-capitalism strategies hold much promise for increasing productivity and spreading the gains from success. They report that roughly one worker in five is involved in some sort of profit-sharing arrangement and that an equivalent fraction of workers own their employer's stock. Although such plans do not automatically improve productivity, they often do. And employee stock ownership plans (ESOPs) appear to increase productivity by perhaps 5 percent and to increase job security somewhat as well.

The authors end with a call for a variety of mechanisms to enhance employer knowledge of high-performance, employee-friendly practices and for continued willingness to use tax incentives to encourage ESOPs and similar methods of employee ownership.

What Should Government Do?

The last two chapters were commissioned as a pair. William Niskanen, a member of Ronald Reagan's Council of Economic Advisers, and Rebecca Blank, a council member under Bill Clinton, were asked to consider whether we should be troubled by the trends in inequality and what, if anything, should be done about them. Their chapters differ significantly in tone and focus, yet, in some respects, what is more striking are the widespread areas of agreement between the two authors.

In chapter 3 Niskanen begins by reviewing what may be causing the changes in work and pay. He emphasizes that we seem to be at the dawn of a new industrial revolution. But he highlights the puzzle that productivity gains have been slow to materialize. Moreover, he discusses the possibility that with technological change and market responses, over time productivity will rise and inequality will decline. He also notes the contribution of trade, immigration, skills, and institutions. He then turns to the question of what should be done.

Niskanen then tackles the question of whether we should care. He notes that a reasonable case can be made that we should not. Clearly he is not bothered much by inequality per se. Still, he is troubled that the least advantaged are becoming worse off. Thus he believes that policy efforts should be directed toward the least skilled.

Niskanen is as clear about what he opposes as about what he favors. He eschews "European model" solutions that he characterizes as centralized wage setting, government restrictions on firing, and generous unemployment benefits of extended duration. He also believes that the nation should oppose restrictive trade or immigration policies, increases in the minimum wage, employer mandates for family leave or medical coverage, and changes in labor law designed to strengthen unions. His orientation is toward removing government barriers that restrict opportunity for the least skilled.

He favors a strong focus on kindergarten through twelfth-grade education with a particular focus on vouchers. His reading of the early evidence is that where school vouchers have been tried, performance has improved. He would improve the process of school-to-work transition but is somewhat skeptical about the various alternatives. Finally, he emphasizes the benefits of the earned income tax credit (EITC), which offers low-income working families a refundable tax credit of up to $3,500, which he views as an essential part of protecting low-income families. And although he opposes any major changes in labor law that would strengthen unions, he believes that something must be done to reverse recent rulings that create obstacles to attempts by companies to form quality circles, one of the high-performance workplace features that Kruse and Blasi discuss.

In chapter 4 Blank spends considerable time examining why we should care. Some of her points parallel implicit themes in Niskanen's chapter. She cites wage declines as a signal of productivity declines, which she too finds worrisome. And she worries about declines in well-being of the least skilled and their families. But Blank goes further to worry about devaluing employment and lessening civic cohesion. Although the two authors start from very different perspectives, they agree that the primary emphasis ought to be on the problems of the least skilled more than on inequality per se.

When it comes to policy, Blank and Niskanen have some areas in common. Blank also wants to focus on kindergarten through twelfth-grade education. She would look beyond vouchers and consider a variety of other proposals, but she thinks it sensible to experiment with vouchers as one tool for improving schooling. She too thinks that school-to-work programs should be considered. Blank goes further in calling for enhanced public and private training, although she recognizes its limits. And she points to the potentially important issue of creating better job ladders for less-skilled workers. Just like Niskanen, Blank emphasizes the importance of the EITC, opposes trade protectionism, and thinks that serious union expansion in its current form is unlikely. Thus in major ways these two authors find common ground.

However, the two part company on the question of minimum wages and employment subsidies for health care or wages. Blank is comfortable with limited demand-side strategies such as highly targeted, time-limited public service employment. And she speculates about what sorts of new institutional structures involving worker organization and management might improve the current situation.

The Bigger Picture and Future Directions

It is interesting to reflect on what all these chapters collectively imply about work, inequality, and policy. After talking at length about the information contained in these chapters as well as listening to other presentations, the members of the DSG emerged with a strong conviction that a variety of pressures, from expanded technology to trade to a far more demanding group of investors, have created a far more competitive marketplace. This has placed dramatically greater demands on both workers and employers. The old rules no longer apply—employees can no longer count on secure jobs so long as they work hard and are loyal to the company. And employers may have to work especially hard to keep their most valuable employees. Most workers seem more likely to move between several—even many—jobs over their careers. That greater job mobility imposes both costs in terms of lost income and benefits as well as opportunities for advancement. The group most disadvantaged by these changes are the least-skilled male workers, whose jobs have vanished and been replaced by lower-paying ones, whose internal job ladders have been lost, and for whom job mobility may not lead to real growth in incomes.

At least some members of the group felt that American industry was at something of a crossroads. Business-as-usual no longer works. Firms face a choice: they can take the high road by adopting high-performance workplace strategies that create a loyal and flexible workplace. Or they can take the low road by treating employees like any other item in the inventory, minimizing costs in every way, and using just-in-time hiring strategies where workers are hired only as needed and let go quickly when the market or product mix changes. There are clear examples of both strategies in the economy. Many in the group worried that the high road was most likely to be taken by high-technology and high-wage firms with a highly skilled workforce, while more and more less-skilled workers would be found in low-road jobs without real job ladders or security. There was considerable discussion, but also real discomfort, with the idea that the government might want to reward high-road employers and penalize low-road ones.

Everyone seemed troubled by the fortunes of the least skilled. And not unlike Blank and Niskanen, it was the struggles of this group, more than inequality per se, that people found troubling. Still there was considerable concern that job changing and the diminished security of middle-class workers were worrisome as well.

The group did agree wholeheartedly with many of the common policy recommendations of Blank and Niskanen. Everyone seemed convinced that the EITC was critically important and should be protected from budget cuts. Everyone was equally convinced that elementary and secondary education need to be improved and that we should be willing to experiment far more widely, although vouchers were controversial with some.

The most interesting feature of the discussion was the enthusiasm for investigating new directions. First, the group felt it essential for the nation to generate real mobility and usable skills. Beyond a focus on education and training, the group was excited by an idea advanced by Katherine Newman that the nation might be able to find ways to create more effective job ladders between firms. Then lower-paid employees who perform well in one short-term job could use that solid work performance to move into a better and more secure job in the future. Indeed, this issue was the focus of a recent two-day meeting of the group in New York.

Second, the group wanted to explore ways to make jobs work for everyone. That requires thinking hard as people move from job to job when benefits have traditionally been tied to long-term employment. We need to maintain a highly mobile labor market without creating unreasonably high levels of insecurity for workers. Thus issues like portability of benefits and even some decoupling of benefits from employment merit examination. It is important to think about the binds of work and family time that are created by the fact that all the adults in a household often work. And it is important to have the government continue to offer and even expand supports for low-income working families—from health coverage to child care to other supports, including the EITC.

The chapters in this volume are the beginning of still more work to come. We hope and expect that they narrow the range of disagreement and uncertainty and point toward possible directions for the future.

Chapter 1

Winners and Losers in America: Taking the Measure of the New Economic Realities

IN THE cacophony of voices characterizing the U.S. economy, it is easy to get confused. To some, "We are watching the beginnings of a global boom on a scale never experienced before . . . riding the early waves of a twenty-five-year run of a greatly expanding economy that will do much to solve seemingly intractable problems like poverty" (Schwartz and Leyden 1977, 113). Yet other commentators claim, "The typical American family is worse off in the mid-1990s than it was at the end of the 1970s" (Mishel, Bernstein, and Schmitt 1997, 4). Wage dispersion is said to be growing dramatically and male wages to be falling. Still others argue, "Instead of experiencing substantial deterioration, workers have on average continued to realize small gains in their total compensation" (Kosters 1997, 20). How are we to understand these seemingly discordant voices? Is this a problem of data? Of a glass half full or half empty? Or is Alan Blinder correct that the U.S. economy is like "the Little Girl with the Little Curl" who "when she was good, she was very, very, good, but when she was bad she was *horrid*" (presentation at the August 1997 Aspen Institute's Domestic Strategy Group meeting).

The potential for confusion is neatly illustrated by comparing two measures of economic performance: national income per person and the median annual earnings of full-year, full-time male workers. Those two measures are shown on figure 1.1. National income per person (per capita) is published by the Bureau of Economic Analysis (the source of most official data on things like gross national product) as part of the national income and product accounts (NIPA), and it is meant to capture the entirety of income and compensation generated in the nation, including wages, benefits, profits, rents, interest, and the like. National income per person is precisely the amount of money that

2   A Working Nation

Figure 1.1   Real National Income per Person and Real Median Earnings of Full-Year, Full-Time Male Workers, 1961 to 1995 (Constant Dollars)

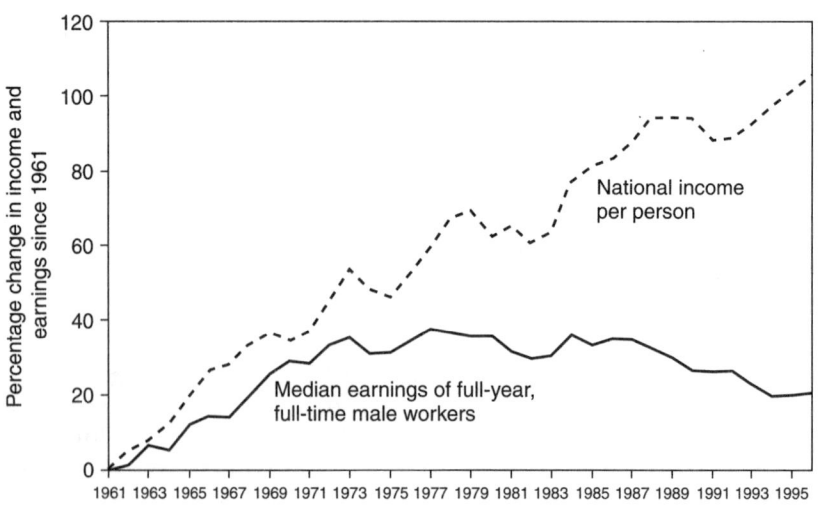

Source: BEA data and annual March CPS data.
Note: National income data are adjusted using the PCE; median earnings data are adjusted using the CPI-U-X1.

could be given to every man, woman, and child if all the income produced by the economy were divided equally. Figure 1.1 shows robust growth in this measure throughout the period. It grew slightly faster in the 1960s than in later periods, but even after several dips during recessions, growth has been steadily upward. Between the critical years of 1973 (a peak year) and 1996 (another very good year), national income per person rose 34 percent.

The median earnings of full-year, full-time male workers are available from the Bureau of the Census, and they often are taken as a measure of pay levels. They show what fully employed male workers are earning. One might expect national income per capita to track median earnings of men pretty closely. Most income is from earnings; most earnings are still paid to men. Yet this measure shows a dramatically different pattern. After rising with national income in the 1960s, median earnings of full-time male workers leveled off and even started falling. Indeed, according to this figure, they declined 10 percent between 1973 and 1996.

These two seemingly inconsistent patterns—a rise of 34 percent and a decline of 10 percent—can in fact be reconciled, illustrating some of the most important patterns in the American economy. Both patterns capture important elements of the larger national picture of income, work, pay, and family.

To begin with, the trends are somewhat misleading for several reasons. The series on median income of full-year, full-time workers suffers from an overly pessimistic adjustment for inflation, which may create the impression that things got worse than they actually did. Instead of the 10 percent decline in median male earnings from 1973 to 1996 that is shown on figure 1.1, median earnings would rise a slight 1 percent using what I regard as a more reasonable correction for inflation.[1] Of course, having no growth in the median man's real earnings over a nearly twenty-five-year period still presents a troubling picture of the American economy.

It turns out that national income per capita as shown on figure 1.1 also suffers from a pessimistic inflation adjustment. A more reasonable measure of inflation would have shown not the 35 percent increase between 1973 and 1996 found on table 1.1, but rather a 50 percent rise! So simply changing the inflation adjustment does nothing to resolve the puzzle: it makes both trends look better, but they are still quite different.

National income per person also suffers another problem for my purpose. If, as actually occurred between the 1960s and 1980s, the number of children per adult falls dramatically, then national income per person will rise even if the adults are earning no more money.[2] The same money is being shared with fewer children, and national income *per person* rises. The decline in children does mean that adults can keep a bit more income, but not because the economy is doing better. It makes far more sense to look at national income *per adult* if we are wondering how well the economy is generating income. This demographic change reduces the apparent growth in national income. If we make both corrections (better adjustments for inflation and better measures of national income per adult), national income per adult rose 35 percent. The two corrections essentially offset one another.

Still most of the puzzle remains: national income per adult apparently rose 35 percent between 1973 and 1996, but median earnings of fully employed males stagnated. How can this be? Virtually the entire story can be seen on table 1.1, which decomposes national income per adult into various components. Over the past twenty-three years, national income per adult rose $8,278. Where did that money go?

- Roughly $2,660 went to greater profits, interest, rent, and proprietors' income. This was a rise of 40 percent.

4   A Working Nation

Table 1.1   National Income per Adult and Components, 1973 and 1996 (1996 U.S. Dollars Unless Otherwise Noted)

	1973	1996	Absolute Change	Percentage Change
Total national income per adult	23,703	31,981	8,278	35
Component				
Profits, rents, proprietor's income, and net interest	6,683	9,345	2,662	40
Total compensation for female wage and salary workers[a]				
Women with wages in top one-third	2,331	4,792	2,461	106
Women with wages in middle one-third	1,261	2,263	1,001	79
Women with wages in bottom one-third	472	904	432	92
Total compensation for male wage and salary workers[a]				
Men with wages in top one-third	7,136	9,127	1,991	28
Men with wages in middle one-third	4,123	3,985	−138	−3
Men with wages in bottom one-third	1,694	1,564	−130	−8

Source: Published NIPA data and author's tabulations of CPS data.
Note: All figures are per adult age eighteen and over and adjusted by the PCE less 0.5 percent per year.
[a] Includes employer-paid benefits and supplements and adjustments to make the CPS and NIPA data comparable.

- Much of the money went to greater compensation for women, including $2,461 (a 106 percent rise) for women in the top third of wages, $1,001 (a 79 percent rise) for women in the middle third, and $432 (a 92 percent rise) for women in the bottom third. Much of this increase was caused by the fact that women worked more outside the home in 1996 than they did in 1973.
- Roughly $1,990 went for extra compensation to men in the top third.
- Essentially nothing went to men in the middle third, and men at the bottom actually received less.

It seems, then, that

- Many groups gained economically in the period 1973 to 1996: women overall, capital holders, and higher-wage men—nearly all, it seems, *except the bottom two-thirds of men*. So there is nothing inconsistent in the two trends on figure 1.1 at all. Earnings of men in the middle—captured properly by *median* male earnings—did not rise. But national income, which includes the money everyone else was gaining, grew steadily.
- Since virtually all of the capital is held by persons in the top third of households and since the biggest gains in income were for wage earners in the top third, roughly 85 percent of the gains in national income went either to people in the top third of wages or to families.
- By 1996 the total compensation for men in the bottom two-thirds of the wage distribution amounted to just 17 percent of national income.

It simply is not true that middle- and working-class men get much of the income generated in our nation. They never have earned a large share of it, and they are earning less of it each year. Part of the change is the result of greater earnings by women. And some is the result of higher pay to upper-income men and greater earnings by capital.

These results imply that economic changes created greater income and wage dispersion among workers and families, generating strains on families, gender relations, and political institutions. The figures raise as many questions as they answer. Did women work more for the same pay, or did their wages rise while men's were stagnant? Is capital suddenly taking a larger share, or is it taking the same share of a bigger pie? We have the puzzle of stagnant earnings of most men. What has all this meant for families? Unfortunately (except for people who love to talk about statistical methods), if we are to understand some of the controversy about how the economy is doing, we have to start by talking about inflation adjustments. So that is where we begin.

Inflation Adjustments and Why They Matter

Consider the following thought experiment.[3] Suppose one could implement a program that would boost the overall economy 25 percent, but only very unevenly, so that the top third had a rise in income of 50 percent, while the bottom two-thirds had a fall in income of 10 percent. Would one favor such a plan? Is it fair for some to gain a lot, while many others lose a little? Some would go for the bigger pie. But many would have a hard time endorsing such a program. Suppose instead that an alternative program would boost the economy overall 35 percent. The gains would again be shared very unevenly, with those in the top third getting a 50 percent increase and those in the bottom two-thirds getting nothing. Would one favor that plan? No one is getting "hurt" except in the sense that their incomes are failing to keep pace with those of others. Or let us take things a step further, what if we could get 50 percent growth with a 65 percent increase in income for the top and a 10 percent increase for the middle and bottom? Again the gap between the rich and the rest is growing dramatically, but this time everyone is at least gaining something. At a minimum most people would regard the third scenario far more favorably than the first.

It is possible to claim that any one of these three scenarios roughly corresponds to the American economy of the past twenty-five years, depending on the adjustments one makes for inflation. Looking back over the past quarter century, the data show that the economy grew and that the position of those at the top improved relative to the position of those at the bottom. But how much growth there was, and whether the bottom was losing money or simply gaining it more slowly, depends heavily on the answer to one crucial question—how do we adjust for inflation?

The issue boils down to comparing the value of a dollar received roughly twenty-five years ago to the value of a dollar received today. Is a worker earning $30,000 today better or worse off than a worker who earned $10,000 in 1973? If inflation was low in the interim, today's worker might be far better off than his counterpart. But if inflation was high, $30,000 may indeed buy far less now than $10,000 did back then.

There is no theoretically correct way of measuring inflation even if one had perfect information because the goods available and the buying patterns of people are different today than they were in 1973. Some goods such as personal computers simply did not exist in 1973. In other cases, the quality of what people buy has changed—most cars now get far more miles per gallon than they did in the past. In other situations, people have altered their buying habits in response to changing prices or tastes. If one simply priced what was bought in 1973 at 1996 prices, one surely would overstate inflation. Since people are not choosing to make the same purchases as they did in 1973, they must believe that they can use the same money to buy a different combination of goods and be better off than they would be by sticking with their old buying habits. And plenty of items available in 1973 cannot be found at any reasonable price today, anyway.

So what are government statisticians to do? They try to make adjustments for changes in quality and buying patterns. But such adjustments are notoriously hard to make. Over the years improvements have been made, and these adjustments tend to show less inflation than the earlier methods implied. Some claim that the standard index—the current price index (CPI)—still significantly overstates inflation. Recently the Boskin Commission, set up by Congress, concluded that the current index overstates inflation by perhaps 1 percentage point a year (Advisory Commission to Study the Consumer Price Index 1996).

Some have been critical of the Boskin report. They argue that, taken to its logical extreme, the report implies that half of the population would have been poor in 1961 (Baker 1997). Other methods of calculating inflation show numbers much closer to the current CPI (for a fascinating alternative approach, see Krueger and Siskind 1997). There is no generally agreed correction at this stage, although very recent changes in how the CPI is calculated may reduce reported inflation by up to 0.5 percent (Kosters 1997, 28). Many economists favor another index—the personal consumption expenditure (PCE) index produced by the Bureau of Economic Analysis, which has somewhat fewer problems.

Appendix table 1A.1 shows what national income per adult and median male earnings would look like under different adjustments for inflation. The choice of inflation adjustment makes a difference. Using the version of the CPI most commonly used by economists, male earnings fell 11 percent between 1973 and 1996, while national income per adult rose 20 percent. At the other extreme, using the PCE less 1 percent, male wages *rose* 12 percent and national income rose more than 50 percent. The ratio of the two in any year always remains the same, since inflation adjustments affect both figures equally. It is easy to see why those who proclaim the economy robust point to national income per capita or male wages adjusted by a smaller inflation correction, while those who see trauma point to the median earnings of men adjusted using the CPI.

In all scenarios there is a very large gap in the growth of national income per capita and the growth of median earnings of full-time male workers. An inflation adjustment suggesting that male wages actually rose slightly also suggests that national income rose even more dramatically. Even under the most favorable scenario, men's wages experienced only very modest growth over a twenty-five-year period.

My own conclusion is that, at least until the past year or so, both the CPI and the PCE overstated inflation. But I am skeptical of claims that the overstatement was as large as 1 percent. Thus for this chapter, I use PCE less 0.5 percent for the entire period (the shaded figures in table 1A.1). I am somewhat hesitant to deviate from the official inflation indexes that paint a more pessimistic picture, but I think this level of adjustment is justified. The remainder of the chapter and table 1.1

make this adjustment. The puzzle to be resolved is how and why real national income per adult could rise 35 percent, while male earnings were flat.

The adjustment does not affect many of the conclusions, particularly those regarding rising inequality or where the bulk of the new money went. But the absolute levels of growth or decline in wages, profits, or benefits do hinge on the inflation adjustment. And depending on the inflation adjustment used, one observer's modest fall in wages can be translated into another's modest rise. For those unhappy with this particular assumption regarding inflation, I have reproduced several of the key tables in the appendix using the official inflation adjustments.

A Word About Data Sources

Another difficulty in interpreting the various data series is that they come from different sources. Aggregate data on things like national income, total compensation, and profits are produced by the Bureau of Economic Analysis and published in the national income and product accounts. The Bureau of Economic Analysis uses a variety of data sources and imputations to derive estimates of aggregate economic performance. These data are not available on anything like an individual level. Thus one can see how much was paid in total compensation, but not how much of that compensation went for men versus women or high-wage versus low-wage workers.

By far the best annual source of individual data is the current population survey (CPS). Each month data are collected on employment and unemployment, and CPS data are used to produce the official unemployment statistics released each month. In March of each year, additional questions are asked regarding the annual sources and amounts of income of each family member, the number of weeks and hours worked during the year, and the like. This information is collected along with information on education, age, race, sex, marital status, family makeup, and the like for a very large sample of Americans. CPS data are used for much of the study of income and work patterns. Unfortunately, CPS data do not include reliable estimates of the cost of work-related benefits such as pensions or health coverage. They have little information on profits not distributed as dividends, and they lack some other factors as well. Thus one cannot simply add up all the income reported in the CPS and get the same aggregate national income as reported in the NIPA.

In this chapter, I seek to understand where the aggregate money went, and thus I am required to work with both NIPA and CPS data.

This creates the need to explain a few anomalies and make some corrections along the way. In general, though, with minor adjustments, it is not too difficult to make the individual data from the CPS line up with the aggregate data of NIPA sufficiently to understand what is happening in the American economy.

Male Earnings

I turn now to a more detailed examination of what happened with male earnings. For my analysis of wages, I rely heavily on CPS data. I start by looking only at work, wages, and earnings (excluding benefits) as reported in the CPS. As shown on table 1.1 aggregate wage and salary payments rose for males in the top third and were stable or declined for men in the bottom two-thirds. Any changes in aggregate wage and salary payments must be caused by a combination of changes in the number of hours men worked, by changes in wage rates, and by variations in work-related benefits. Table 1.2 shows what happened to the work and wages of men using the CPS.

- Work patterns overall among men did not change much. The fraction of adult men who worked at all during the year fell roughly 5 percent between 1973 and 1996, but this was partially offset by a 2 percent increase in hours among those who did work.
- Wage changes among men were highly unequal. Wages of men in the top third rose 27 percent, those of the middle third rose just 1 percent, and those of men in the bottom third declined 4 percent.

The lack of growth for median workers does not show what happened to individuals over time. Most men still got higher pay as they aged (for a wonderful chart showing what happened to individuals and families in a cohort as they aged, see Levy 1996). The results here imply that sons typically earned no more than their fathers did at a comparable age. Table 1.2 reveals very powerful patterns by education and age:

- Wage changes varied dramatically by level of education. Over the roughly twenty-five years, the wages for the least-educated men fell 24 percent, while wages of men at the top educational levels rose a comparable amount.
- Wages of younger men fell during this period, while wages of men in the upper age groups rose. The rise in pay of older men can be explained in part by the fact that sharp rises in education in the 1930s and 1940s led to a far more educated older workforce in the 1990s

Table 1.2 Wages of Men, 1973 and 1996 (1996 U.S. Dollars Unless Otherwise Noted)

Indicator	1973	1996	Absolute Change	Percentage Change
Fraction of adult men who worked at all during the year	0.77	0.73	−0.04	−5
Average hours worked per week by men who worked	37.6	38.5	0.9	2
Mean wage by wage thirds[a]				
Men in the top one-third of wages	24.11	30.62	6.51	27
Men in the middle one-third of wages	12.77	12.93	0.17	1
Men in the bottom one-third of wages	6.75	6.45	−0.30	−4
Median wage by education				
More than college	19.32	24.23	4.92	25
College graduate	16.46	17.31	0.85	5
Some post–high school	12.79	12.50	−0.29	−2
High school graduate	12.66	11.54	−1.12	−9
Less than high school	10.40	7.93	−2.47	−24
Median wage by education				
Men age eighteen to twenty-four	8.00	6.97	−1.02	−13
Men age twenty-five to thirty-four	13.17	11.54	−1.63	−12
Men age thirty-five to forty-four	15.20	14.90	−0.29	−2
Men age forty-five to fifty-four	15.20	16.78	1.58	10
Men age fifty-five to sixty-four	13.42	15.32	1.89	14
Median wage by race				
White men	12.79	12.98	0.19	1
African American men	9.14	10.55	1.41	15
Spanish ethnicity men	n.a.	8.50	n.a.	n.a.

Source: Author's tabulations of CPS data.
Note: All figures are per adult age eighteen and over and adjusted by the PCE less 0.5 percent per year.
[a] Calculated using aggregate earnings divided by aggregate hours for the group.

than in the 1970s. But the fall in pay for the young is surprising given the fact that they are comparatively well educated.

- African American men gained relative to whites. While median wages of white men were stagnant, those for black men rose 15 percent. Blacks still earned nearly 20 percent less than whites did in 1996. And Latino men earned dramatically less. This result should be interpreted quite cautiously, for it is one of the few in this chapter that seem quite sensitive to the data source used. Other data series tend to show that black and white wages changed about equally over this period. I cannot explain this discrepancy (which is also noted without explanation in Council of Economic Advisers 1998, 144).

Tables 1.1 and 1.2 seem to offer a compelling explanation for what has been called "the angry white male" phenomenon. Wages of white men in the bottom two-thirds stagnated or fell, while the fortunes of many others improved. Coupled with the rising economic independence of women and the recent strength of corporate profits, it is easy to see how the message of a Pat Buchanan would hold such sway. The results also have profound implications for families. The ages between eighteen and forty-four are the period when family formation and child rearing chiefly occur. If younger middle-class men are faring poorly, this creates pressures for children. I return to this issue in a later section.

Confusion is sometimes introduced into this debate by focusing on mean rather than median wages. Mean wage figures are dominated heavily by the earnings of men at the top, since the bulk of income goes to them. Mean wages can rise sharply even if the wages of median workers remain unchanged. Indeed even though table 1.2 shows essentially no change in wages of workers in the middle and a fall for those below, the mean wage for all men rose 16 percent (not shown). That properly reflects the fact that there was a 16 percent increase in total monies paid to men. Unfortunately, virtually all that money went to men in the top third of the income distribution. If one cares about how much money the economy is generating overall, then mean wages are helpful. But if one cares about what is happening to workers themselves, the median or a measure of pay for different groups is more useful.

So far I have looked chiefly at two points in time. But more can be learned by looking over the entire period of 1961 to 1996. Perhaps the best data series over this period examines the earnings of full-year, full-time male workers at different spots on the wage distribution. I focus particularly on the group where schooling is completed and also the period when the bulk of child rearing traditionally occurs. Figure 1.2 plots the percentage change since 1961 in wages for workers at various

Figure 1.2 Percentage Change in Earnings of Full-Year, Full-Time Male Workers by Percentile, 1961 to 1995

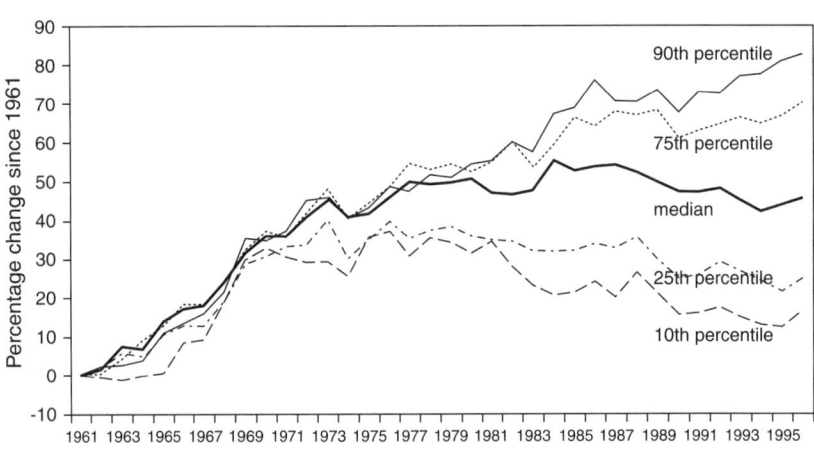

Source: BEA data and annual March CPS data.
Note: Real dollars adjusted for inflation using PCE less 0.5 percent per year.

parts of the earnings distribution. By looking at percentage changes, I can examine whether men's wages at different levels were moving together or apart. If a rising tide lifts all boats, one would expect to see the same percentage changes in the wages of people at all levels of the distribution. But if some groups were gaining more than others, the lines would diverge. The figure shows the following:

- The 1960s and early 1970s were a time of *shared prosperity*—wages of men at all levels rose together. The latter 1970s seemed to be a time of *shared stagnation* among men, with wages of most groups leveling off, although there was some divergence at the bottom. But starting around 1980, patterns began to diverge sharply. Wages for those at the top began to grow, while pay for those at the bottom fell precipitously. The 1980s and 1990s were a time of *divergent prosperity and decline*.
- Men in the top saw significant rises in pay. Those at the bottom in 1996 had pay that was well below the level of comparable men in 1973.

Thus far I have looked only at levels of pay. For many purposes, it is important to look at total compensation, including benefits and social insurance contributions, not just wages. Indeed, employees understand that health insurance and pension funds are a critical part

Table 1.3 Fraction of Male Workers at Different Wage Levels with Health and Pension Benefits, 1979 and 1996

Indicator	Percentage with Employer- or Union-Supported Health Benefits		Percentage with Employer- or Union-Supported Pension Benefits	
	1979	1996	1979	1996
Men in the top one-third of the wage distribution	85	78	76	71
Men in the middle one-third of the wage distribution	77	64	60	53
Men in the bottom one-third of the wage distribution	42	32	24	19
All men	68	58	53	48

Source: Author's tabulations of CPS data.

of their total compensation. In addition, employers are responsible for paying taxes on the employee's behalf for social security, medicare, and unemployment insurance. Some may argue that social insurance taxes should not be counted as employee compensation, but they are real costs for employers, and the *employee's* contributions for social insurance are counted here as part of his or her gross pay. It is possible that benefits and contributions are equalizers, reducing the apparent disparity in pay.

Benefit costs have risen sharply both absolutely and as a fraction of total pay: whereas aggregate employer-paid supplements effectively added an additional 15 percent to wage payments of employers in 1973, by 1996 they added 22 percent. About half of the employer-paid supplements was for benefits like health and pensions. The other half was for social insurance and payroll tax payments. This fraction changed little over the years because health costs rose rapidly along with payroll taxes for social security and medicare.

Individual-level data indicating who receives health and pension benefits are available on a consistent basis from the CPS only since 1979. Table 1.3 shows the fraction of male workers at various wage levels who were getting employer-provided health coverage and pension benefits. The fraction of men getting benefits of each type fell over this period for workers at all levels, but declines were greatest among those at the bottom. Declines in health benefits were particularly dramatic. Whereas 42 percent of male workers in the bottom third had health benefits in

1979, less than a third had such benefits in 1996. Pension benefits also fell sharply for this group.

Thus benefits, just like pay, became significantly more unequal over time. Given that all male groups saw a loss in coverage, it may seem surprising that aggregate national benefit costs grew at all. Some of this rise was for more coverage of women, who worked more and became more likely to qualify for benefits. The rest was the result of rising health costs. The costs of health coverage rose so fast that even with falling coverage total costs were up.[4]

Unlike health and pension benefits, social insurance contributions are skewed slightly toward lower-wage workers. Employers contribute a constant share of earnings up to a limit for social security and medicare. (Since 1993 there has been no limit on medicare contributions.) Employer contributions have risen faster than earnings over the years as both the amount of covered earnings and the tax rate have risen steadily.[5]

It would be helpful to add these wage supplements to wages to calculate what happened to total compensation of workers at various levels. Unfortunately, CPS data do not include information on the individual costs of these supplements. Moreover, they do not even have information on who received such benefits before 1979. NIPA data are available on the aggregate annual costs of health, pension, social insurance, and several other employer-paid supplements well into the past. But only national aggregates are available. With some modest assumptions (including the assumption that there was little change in the pattern of coverage between 1973 and 1979), we can estimate the value of such benefits separately for men and women and for different income groups.[6] These are shown on table 1.4. The effect of adding wage supplements is to exacerbate the growing disparity in wages, not narrow it. The value of wage supplements grew far more in both absolute and percentage terms for men in the top third than for men in the bottom third.

One other imputation seems appropriate for accurately tracking what happened to the pay of men at different levels over time. Table 1.1 sought to track various components of national income. National income totals are available only from NIPA data. Included in the NIPA series is a measure of aggregate wage and salary earnings. CPS data are an alternative source of wage and salary earnings. NIPA data are based largely on wage reporting to public agencies for unemployment insurance purposes. There are legal consequences to misreporting such data. CPS data, in contrast, come from surveys of individuals, and there are no legal consequences for errors. More important, until recently, CPS surveys did not always make it absolutely clear to respondents that

Table 1.4 Work and Wages of Men with Benefits Imputed and Correction for CPS Underreporting, 1973 and 1996 (1996 U.S. Dollars Unless Otherwise Noted)

Indicator	1973	1996	Absolute Change	Percentage Change
Men in the top one-third of the wage distribution				
CPS wages	24.11	30.62	6.51	27
Imputed employer-paid benefits	3.50	6.41	2.91	83
CPS correction to match NIPA	1.55	−0.15	−1.70	
Total hourly compensation	29.16	36.88	7.72	26
Men in the middle one-third of the wage distribution				
CPS wages	12.77	12.93	0.17	1
Imputed employer-paid benefits	2.19	3.04	0.85	39
CPS under- or over-reporting Correction	0.82	−0.06	−0.89	
Total hourly compensation	15.78	15.91	0.13	1
Men in the bottom one-third of the wage distribution				
CPS wages	6.75	6.45	−0.30	−4
Imputed employer-paid benefits	1.00	1.21	0.22	22
CPS correction to match NIPA	0.43	−0.03	−0.47	
Total hourly compensation	8.18	7.63	−0.55	−7

Source: Published NIPA data and author's tabulations of CPS data.
Note: All figures are per adult age eighteen and over and adjusted by the PCE less 0.5 percent per year.

what was sought were earnings *before any tax or benefit withholding*. There is ample reason to believe that income was underreported on the CPS until recently. As shown on figure 1A.1 in the appendix, aggregate CPS wage and salary income was invariably less than NIPA's totals until recently. In 1973, for example, CPS aggregate income was 7 percent less than NIPAs. With a variety of improvements in the reporting of each series, CPS and NIPA data now show virtually identical totals—differing by only one half of 1 percent. Even the 7 percent difference in 1973 does not sound like a lot, but it does affect the trends significantly. If earlier CPS data suffer underreporting, then earnings in 1973 should have been 7 percent higher (for an excellent discussion of the problems with different wage series, and which series might be best to use where, see Abraham, Spletzer, and Stewart 1997).

Logically, both wage supplements and an adjustment for likely CPS underreporting should be included with wages in determining the overall pattern in compensation. Table 1.4 shows the effects of adding both to hourly compensation. The effects partially offset one another. Benefits grow over time, but the correction declines. Ultimately, the figures on table 1.4 show much the same pattern seen in wages alone.

When one examines total compensation, including all benefits and wage supplements, and adjusts for probable CPS underreporting in earlier years, compensation of men in the top third grew 26 percent, compensation for those in the middle third was flat, and pay for those in the bottom third fell 7 percent in the past quarter century.

It is worth pausing to explore the effect of alternative inflation adjustments. By applying the usual CPI adjustment that is used in most official reports, male compensation for the middle third actually fell 11 percent (instead of rising 1 percent as shown here) in the past twenty-three years, and compensation for males at the bottom declined 17 percent. Using the CPI less 1 percent, as some have argued, median male compensation instead rose 11 percent, and workers at the bottom broke roughly even. Of course, under this most optimistic scenario, the wages of men at the top rose much more dramatically also, a full 40 percent.

Between 1973 and 1996, under almost any scenario, the wages of men in the middle changed relatively little—modest rises or falls are possible depending on the inflation and other adjustments. And under any scenario, those workers in the top third did much better and those at the bottom did the worst. No matter what inflation adjustment is used, one fact is undeniable. Wage disparities among men rose dramatically over the past twenty to twenty-five years. Men in the bottom two-thirds of the wage distribution earned a significantly smaller share of national income in 1996 than they did in 1973.

The Changing Earnings of Female Workers

Table 1.1 shows that aggregate earnings of women were rising from 1973 to 1996. What we do not know is whether this increase was primarily due to women working more or women receiving higher wages. Tables 1.5, 1.6, and 1.7 and figure 1.3 present results comparable to the earlier ones for men.

In sharp contrast to men, there were dramatic increases in work by women. Some 24 percent more women worked in the labor market, and average weekly hours among those who did work rose 15 percent. Overall, women contributed 40 percent more work hours in 1996 than they did in 1973.

One can infer the relative significance of greater work versus higher pay by comparing the percentage increases in table 1.1 with those in

Table 1.5 Work and Wages of Women, 1973 and 1996
(1996 U.S. Dollars Unless Otherwise Noted)

Indicator	1973	1996	Absolute Change	Percentage Change
Fraction of adult women who worked at all during the year	0.49	0.61	0.12	24
Average hours worked per week by women who worked	27.8	32.0	4.3	15
Mean wage by wage thirds[a]				
Women in the top one-third of wages	13.77	20.68	6.92	50
Women in the middle one-third of wages	7.57	9.83	2.26	30
Women in the bottom one-third of wages	3.96	5.17	1.21	30
Median wage by education				
More than college	13.87	18.33	4.46	32
College graduate	10.50	13.46	2.96	28
Some post–high school	8.26	9.62	1.36	16
High school graduate	7.45	8.17	0.72	10
Less than high school	5.95	6.12	0.17	3
Median wage by race				
White women	7.63	9.61	1.98	26
African American women	6.42	8.63	2.21	34
Spanish ethnicity women	n.a.	7.50	n.a.	n.a.
Median wage by age				
All women age eighteen to twenty-four	6.29	6.15	−0.14	−2
All women age twenty-five to thirty-four	8.32	9.62	1.29	16
All women age thirty-five to forty-four	8.00	10.82	2.82	35
All women age forty-five to fifty-four	8.17	11.06	2.89	35
All women age fifty-five to sixty-four	7.86	9.94	2.08	26

Source: Published NIPA data and author's tabulations of CPS data.
Note: All figures are per adult age eighteen and over and adjusted by the PCE less 0.5 percent per year.
[a] Calculated using aggregate earnings divided by aggregate hours for the group.

Table 1.6 Fraction of Female Workers at Different Wage Levels with Health and Pension Benefits, 1979 and 1996

Indicator	Percentage with Employer- or Union-Supported Health Benefits		Percentage with Employer- or Union-Supported Pension Benefits	
	1979	1996	1979	1996
Women in the top one-third of the wage distribution	67	67	65	61
Women in the middle one-third of the wage distribution	53	54	46	40
Women in the bottom one-third of the wage distribution	28	24	17	16
All women	49	48	43	39

Source: Author's tabulations of CPS data.

table 1.5. For each wage group, earnings grew more than twice as fast as wages—thus rising work accounted for at least half of the higher level of women's earnings in national income. Yet, in contrast to men, women at all levels showed at least some rise in wages between 1973 and 1996. Even women in the bottom third of wages averaged a 30 percent rise in the rate of pay.

As shown on table 1.6, the fraction of female workers with benefits fell, but not nearly as much as for men, undoubtedly because women were working longer and qualifying for more benefits. And given that the number of women working increased sharply over this period, a fairly constant share of a rising pool implies a significant increase in benefits as well as pay for women at nearly all levels.

Comparing table 1.2 for men with table 1.5 for women, one finds that women still earn significantly less than men. The median female earns only 76 percent of what the median male does. At every educational level, women's pay is lower. But at every level, the gains of women were greater than those of men in the past quarter century, so the gap narrowed.

The results remain something of a puzzle. One would normally expect that if women chose to work in much larger numbers than before, either because they sought the benefits of work or because they felt economic pressure to do so, their wages would fall relative to the wages of other workers. Yet it is the pay of middle- and working-class men that stagnated. Part of the answer can be traced to the increased work experience of women. As women work more, they accumulate more work experience, and employers are willing to pay them more.

Table 1.7 Work and Wages of Women with Benefits Imputed and Adjustments for CPS Underreporting of Men, 1973 and 1996 (1996 U.S. Dollars Unless Otherwise Noted)

Indicator	1973	1996	Absolute Change	Percentage Change
Women in the top one-third of the wage distribution				
CPS wages	13.77	20.68	6.92	50
Imputed employer-paid benefits	2.38	4.80	2.41	101
CPS correction to match NIPA	0.88	−0.10	−0.99	
Total hourly compensation	17.03	25.37	8.34	49
Women in the middle one-third of the wage distribution				
CPS wages	7.57	9.83	2.26	30
Imputed employer-paid benefits	1.20	2.20	1.00	83
CPS correction to match NIPA	0.49	−0.05	−0.54	
Total hourly compensation	9.26	11.98	2.72	29
Women in the bottom one-third of the wage distribution				
CPS wages	3.96	5.17	1.21	30
Imputed employer-paid benefits	0.55	0.91	0.35	64
CPS correction to match NIPA	0.25	−0.03	−0.28	
Total hourly compensation	4.77	6.05	1.28	27

Source: Published NIPA data and author's tabulations of CPS data.
Note: All figures are per adult age eighteen and over and adjusted by the PCE less 0.5 percent per year.

Other research shows that roughly one-third to one-half of the increase in wage rates of women over this period can be traced to their greater experience. When one combines the effect of experience on pay with the effect of working more hours, between two-thirds to three-quarters of the rise in the aggregate earnings of women shown on table 1.5 can be traced to greater work—either more hours today or more hours in the past that are rewarded with higher pay for the experience (for an excellent summary of all the changes for women, see Blau 1998).

Still, even after adjusting for greater work and more experience, women's wages gained relative to men's. No one fully understands why. Part of the answer has to do with the changing economy—with its greater emphasis on services and other activities where brawn offers

Figure 1.3 Percentage Change in Earnings of Full-Year, Full-Time Female Workers by Percentile, 1961 to 1995

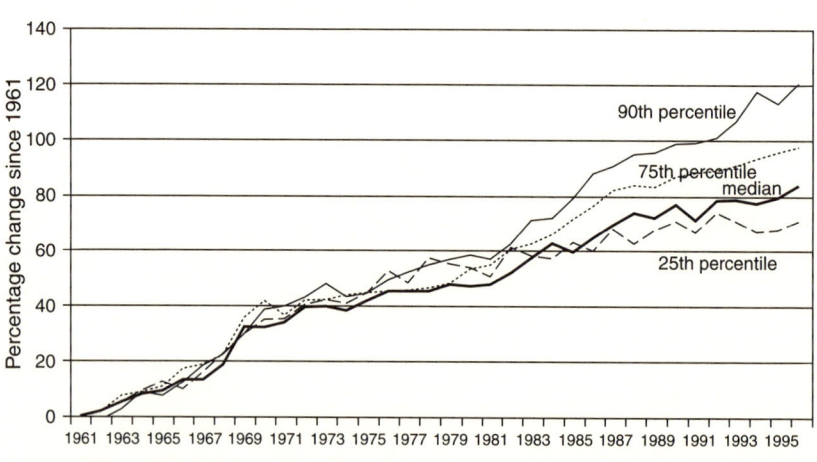

Source: BEA data and annual March CPS data.
Note: Real dollars adjusted for inflation using PCE less 0.5 percent per year.

few advantages. And some may be the result of reduced discrimination and affirmative action.

Even though the basic trends rise far more for women than for men, many features of pay are very similar between men and women. Just as for men, the increase in compensation for women was greatest for those with the most education and those who were highest up in the wage distribution. The highest third of women saw an hourly wage increase of 50 percent. And the rise in pay for women with a college degree or more was three times greater than the rise for women with a high school degree only. Thus wage inequality for women grew dramatically, just as it did for men.

A very big part of the story of the American economy, then, is the rise in the work and pay of women. Yet even for women, the rising tide lifted some boats far more than others.

Returns to Capital and Capitalists

Table 1.1 shows that a collection of items broadly labeled returns to capital increased fairly dramatically in the past quarter century. Table 1.8 breaks these down further to show which components of returns to capital changed the most.

Between 1973 and 1996, net interest, corporate profits, and rents all rose faster than national income overall. The rise was particularly dra-

Table 1.8 Components of Capital, Income per Capita, 1973 and 1996 (1996 U.S. Dollars Unless Otherwise Noted)

	1973	1996	Absolute Change	Percentage Change
Total national income	**23,705**	**31,981**	**8,276**	**35**
Component				
Profits, proprietors' income, net interest, and rent	6,683	9,345	2,662	40
Net interest	1,183	2,174	991	84
Corporate profits	2,515	3,763	1,248	50
Rent	540	748	208	38
Proprietors' income	2,445	2,660	215	9
Nonfarm	1,763	2,470	707	40
Farm	683	190	−492	−72
Corporate profits as a percentage of national income	11	12		
Corporate profits plus interest as percentage of national income	16	19		

Source: Published NIPA data.
Note: All figures are per capita and adjusted by the PCE less 0.5 percent per year.

matic for interest, but corporate profits also grew nearly 50 percent. Proprietors' income did not keep pace with national income because of declines in farm proprietors' income. Nonfarm proprietors' income rose at the same rate as national income.

A rise in interest or profit income, in and of itself, means nothing. In a robust capitalist economy, returns to capital will grow along with the overall economy. The real question is whether a shift in economic structure or economic power caused capital to gain at the expense of labor. Figure 1.4 shows corporate profits and corporate profits plus interest as a percentage of national income over the entire period from 1961 to 1996. Corporate profit as a share of national income has grown significantly since the early 1980s, but it still is lower than it was throughout most of the 1960s.[7] The combination of profits plus interest is relatively high by historical standards, but still below the various peak years.

How is this possible? We have seen that profits rose while median male wages stagnated or fell. The answer, of course, is that added dollars went to women and upper-income men. More women were working and earning more dollars. Capital earned its usual profit on those women and on higher-income men. Thus profits went up by about the same amount

Figure 1.4 Before- and After-Tax Profits Relative to Wages Plus Benefits for Workers, 1991 to 1995

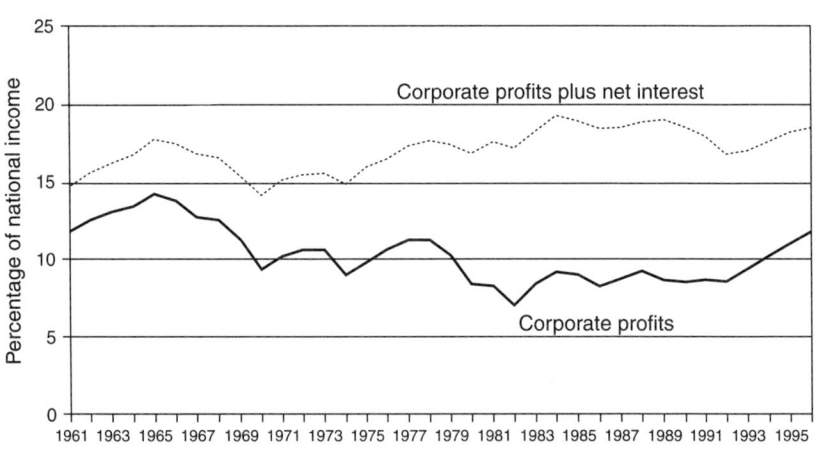

Source: BEA published data.

as total compensation. Another way of looking at this is that capitalists are likely to gain when the number of workers rises. Thus the influx of women into the labor market implies that total profits rose even though the profit rate remained unchanged. There seems to be little support here for claims that most of the change in pay for men was the result of a shift in power to capital. Indeed, such claims would have to account for the rise in pay of women, who presumably had even less power than working men.

Still, the gains to capital owners were quite real. Who benefited from these gains? Since we are looking at the corporate sector here, ownership is principally through stock. Stocks are directly traceable to people when they are held by individuals and pension funds. The owners of that stock are usually quite well-to-do. Adding together individual plus pension holdings reveals that the top 5 percent of households by income own more than half of all stock. The top quarter of families own roughly 85 percent of the total. Thus profit gains accrued almost entirely to higher-income families (Poterba and Samwick 1995).

Several notes of caution need be sounded in this story regarding capital's share. First, the combined total of profits plus interest is very near a fifty-year high. Since owners of capital can hold their money either in stock (and earn shares of profit) or in bonds (and earn interest), it is best to think about capital's share as a combination of stocks and bonds. If current trends continue, capitalists may soon be claiming an unprecedented share of national income. Second, we have talked only about the disposition of national income, not national wealth. Wealth is distributed far more unevenly than income. And the impressive (unrealized) capital gains that stockholders experienced in recent years are not factored into national income. These gains accrued almost entirely to people at the top.

Finally, although profits have not changed much, there is one seemingly anomalous result regarding productivity and pay. Over the years, measures of overall labor productivity have tended to track measures of total compensation quite well. Recently these two trends have diverged somewhat, causing some to argue that capital is gaining at labor's expense. Since profits have not risen much, that is a hard case to make.[8] Instead, the problem seems to be one of price differentials and weak measurement. Economists do not pay much attention to this finding, in part because the measurement of productivity is so problematic. Indeed the measurement of productivity suffers many of the same inevitable problems found in determining an inflation index (firms are producing goods that did not exist previously) along with many others.

Thus what seems to emerge is a story where capital earned healthy but not abnormally high returns in a growing economy where the growth in pay went to women and high-wage men. The story is one of redistribution of pay among workers rather than between capital and labor.

Families and Children

Men's pay was often stagnating while women's earnings were rising. Since families often include both a male and a female, the implications for families and children are somewhat ambiguous. In married couples at least, the rising earnings of women may offset the falling earnings of men, even in the lowest categories. In single-parent families, the rising earnings of women would be expected to help. For this discussion, I focus on families with children.

For much of this discussion I divide families into thirds by looking at education, not income or wage rates. The reason is that income and wages are affected by the decisions that men and women make about working in the home versus working outside it.[9] I group all families with children—both two-parent and single-parent families—into thirds based on the education of the parents. For two-parent families I use the average of both parents' education; for single-parent families, I use the education of the parent the child is living with (and whom we can observe). By dividing all families in this way, when I compare the earnings of women in two-parent families who are in the lower third with those of women in single-parent ones in the bottom third, I am comparing people with similar education. And by breaking education into thirds (rather then looking over time at particular levels of education such as high school graduates), I am looking at comparable shares of parents in each year.

I begin by looking at what happened to two-parent families with children (table 1.9). For each education third, the table shows husband's earnings, wife's earnings, other family income, hours worked by each partner, and mean number of children.

- In two-parent families with children, family income grew at least somewhat in all three parental education categories, rising 14 percent for the bottom third, 25 percent for the middle, and 57 percent for the top.
- The earnings of men roughly paralleled those of men overall, with little or no change for men in the bottom two-thirds and a sizable rise for men in the top third. However, rapidly rising earnings of wives allowed families at all three education levels to increase their income at least somewhat.
- At least half of the rise in earnings of women in each category was due to a dramatic jump in work hours. It seems likely that the work by women was driven in part by a desire to have a rising standard of living when the husband's wages were stagnant. Still, that cannot be the whole story because the rise in work hours was greatest for women in the top category, even though the earnings of the husband were also rising.
- In all parental education groups, the average number of children fell.
- For two-parent families at the top, the combined effect of higher earnings of the husband and much higher earnings of the wife pushed family income ahead far more than for families below them. Thus inequality in family income grew considerably among two-parent families.

The conclusion that two-parent families in all three categories experienced some rise in income must be viewed cautiously. Using the traditional cost of living adjustment would show little or no increase for families at the bottom. Moreover, in each group, at least half of the rise in women's earnings was due to greater work hours. As there was no accompanying decline in male work hours, less time was

Table 1.9 Work and Income for Two-Parent Families with Children by Education Grouping, 1973 and 1996 (1996 U.S. Dollars Unless Otherwise Noted)

Indicator	1973	1996	Absolute Change	Percentage Change
Two-parent families in the top third of parental education[a]				
Husband's earnings	46,140	60,241	14,101	31
Wife's earnings	6,460	21,978	15,518	240
Other family income	3,840	6,409	2,569	67
Total family income	56,440	88,628	32,188	57
Average weekly work hours of husband	43	44	2	4
Average weekly work hours of wife	13	24	12	91
Mean number of children	2.1	1.9	−0.2	−12
Two-parent families in the middle third of parental education[a]				
Husband's earnings	33,968	35,399	1,430	4
Wife's earnings	5,380	13,895	8,515	158
Other family income	3,425	4,170	745	22
Total family income	42,773	53,463	10,690	25
Average weekly work hours of husband	42	42	0	0
Average weekly work hours of wife	14	24	11	78
Mean number of children	2.1	1.9	−0.2	−10
Two-parent families in the bottom third of parental education[a]				
Husband's earnings	25,533	25,620	87	0
Wife's earnings	4,246	9,942	5,696	134
Other family income	5,252	4,326	−926	−18
Total family income	35,032	39,889	4,857	14
Average weekly work hours of husband	38	38	0	−1
Average weekly work hours of wife	12	20	8	64
Mean number of children	2.4	2.0	−0.4	−15

Source: Author's tabulations of the CPS data.
Note: All figures are adjusted by the PCE less 0.5 percent per year.
[a] Calculated based on parental education for both two-parent and single-parent families.

available for care of children, household management, and leisure. Moreover, any greater costs of child care are not reflected here.[10] Finally, in a sizable minority of families in each group, the wife still chose not to work outside the home. Other tabulations show that for two-parent families in the bottom third where the wife was not working, there was a significant fall in family income. Families in this bottom group generally had to send additional workers into the labor market or suffer stagnant or falling living standards in comparison to previous cohorts.

Next, I look next at single parents (including both female and male single parents) using the same educational breaks as before (table 1.10). Because single parents are disproportionately from lower educational backgrounds, 45 percent are in the bottom third of parental education, and only 18 percent are in the top third.

- Single parents in all three educational groups saw at least a small increase in income. Single parents in the top third of parental education saw a sizable rise.

- Earnings rose sharply for women in all groups. But for women in the lower two-thirds of parental education, sharp rises in earnings were offset almost completely by falls in other income. Part of this decrease was a decline in welfare payments, but a large part was a decline in support from others in the household, as single parents became more independent.

One striking feature of table 1.10 is the fact that a large amount of other income was used to support families with low parental education and that support shrank dramatically over time. The origins of this income are many. In 1973 roughly one-third of this support ($3,200) was from welfare. By 1996 welfare support had shrunk dramatically (to $1,200) as a result of falling real benefits, lower participation, and automatic declines imposed on rising earnings. However, in 1973 an even larger amount came from income of others in the household: $4,700, mostly from other relatives such as sisters or parents. By 1996 this amount had shrunk to $1,500, apparently because single parents were more likely to live independently from other relatives. The rest of the outside support was from child support and some other government benefits.

It also is interesting to compare the work behavior of single parents and married mothers.

- At each level of parental education, single parents worked and earned somewhat more than married mothers did. But with little additional income, they had vastly less income than two-parent

Table 1.10 Work and Income for Single-Parent Families with Children by Education Grouping, 1973 and 1996 (1996 U.S. Dollars Unless Otherwise Noted)

Indicator	1973	1996	Absolute Change	Percentage Change
Single-parent families in the top third of parental education[a]				
Head's earnings	17,371	31,917	14,546	84
Other family income	10,365	7,484	−2,881	−28
Total family income	27,735	39,401	11,665	42
Average weekly work hours of head	27	36	9	32
Mean number of children	1.8	1.6	−0.2	−12
Single-parent families in the middle third of parental education[a]				
Head's earnings	11,536	16,738	5,202	45
Other family income	8,480	5,076	−3,404	−40
Total family income	20,017	21,814	1,798	9
Average weekly work hours of head	23	29	5	22
Mean number of children	2.1	1.7	−0.4	−19
Single-parent families in the bottom third of parental education[a]				
Head's earnings	5,704	10,679	4,975	87
Other family income	9,512	5,205	−4,307	−45
Total family income	15,216	15,884	668	4
Average weekly work hours of head	14	22	7	52
Mean number of children	2.4	1.9	−0.6	−24

Source: Author's tabulations of the CPS data.
Note: All figures are adjusted by the PCE less 0.5 percent per year.
[a] Calculated based on parental education for both two-parent and single-parent families.

families. Single parents had less than half of the income of families with two parents for each level of parental education. As a result single-parent families headed by persons in the highest parental education group had lower incomes than two-parent families in the lowest education group.

- The average number of children per single-parent family fell even more sharply than it did among two-parent families.

It is not hard to see why single-parent families are so much more likely to be poor—there is only one potential earner, usually a woman who has low education (nearly half are in the lowest education group) and often works part-time. Other sources of support do not come close to filling the economic gap created by the presence of only one earner. Thus the poverty rate for female single-parent families with children exceeds 40 percent. By contrast, the poverty rate for two-parent families is less than 8 percent.

Fortunately, in each of the broad categories of families examined, there was at least some growth in average income. Unfortunately, that did not translate into rises in income for all children, in part because there was also a sharp increase in the fraction of children in single-parent homes. Children in such homes are invariably poorer than children in comparable two-parent homes. Overall, the fraction of children in single-parent homes rose from 15 to almost 25 percent between 1973 and 1996.

These trends have an important racial dimension. People of color, especially African Americans, are far more likely to be in single-parent homes. What is less well understood, however, is that the growth rate in single-parent homes is greater among whites than blacks. For all races these large changes in family structure imply that family incomes of many children are lower now than when more families had two resident parents.

But changes in family structure are not the only changes that have led some children to be poorer. Recent changes also have hurt two-parent families in the bottom two-thirds where one parent does not work outside the home. The combination of these two factors has hurt the bottom third of children. To see what these changes have wrought, I break children into three groups based on parental income—not education, as before—and look at children in all families simultaneously (table 1.11). A powerful pattern emerges:

- Family incomes for children in the top third rose dramatically between 1973 and 1996, rising nearly 43 percent. Incomes for children in families in the middle grew a modest 9 percent.

- Family incomes for children in the bottom third fell 16 percent. This is the biggest fall seen in this chapter, and it applies to a third of all children! The group at the bottom consists largely of two groups: single-parent families and two-parent families where only one person works.

- As a result of the changes in family structure, the greater earnings gains of wives in high-income families, and the differential earnings

Table 1.11 Family Income and Family Structure for Children by Family Income Groups, 1973 and 1996 (1996 U.S. Dollars Unless Otherwise Noted)

Indicator	1973	1996	Absolute Change	Percentage Change
Children with family income in the top third				
Average family income	69,788	99,855	30,067	43
Fraction of children in two-parent families	0.98	0.96	−0.01	−1
Children with family income in the middle third				
Average family income	36,662	40,053	3,391	9
Fraction of children in two-parent families	0.94	0.84	−0.10	−11
Children with family income in the bottom third				
Average family income	16,673	13,987	−2,686	−16
Fraction of children in two-parent families	0.62	0.43	−0.19	−31

Source: Author's tabulations of the CPS data.
Note: All figures are adjusted by the PCE less 0.5 percent per year.

of men at different parts of the distribution, the distribution of family income widened even more dramatically than the distribution of wages. Families at the top did unusually well. Those at the bottom fell further and further behind.

The worry about such changes is not only that those at the bottom are poorer today. It is also that children in poorer households will have less opportunity in the future. For example, the odds of attending college are tied extremely closely to parental income. A college education is becoming almost essential to achieve growing wages. And perhaps in response, there has been a sharp rise in college attendance lately. But Ellwood and Kane (2000) show that essentially the entire increase in attendance was among children from families in the top 60 percent of income—the place where family incomes are rising. By contrast, college attendance did not rise for children from poorer homes. Those in the bottom are being left further behind.

It seems natural to ask whether the changing economic patterns played some role in the changes in family structure. It seems plausible that the declining or stagnant fortunes of many men, coupled with the increasing earning capacity of women, might make marriage seem less attractive or

Table 1.12 Fraction of Men Age Twenty-Five to Forty-Four Who Are Married and Living with Their Spouse by Education Grouping, 1973 and 1996

Indicator	1973	1996	Absolute Change	Percentage Change
Top third of education	0.79	0.64	−0.15	−19
Middle third of education	0.80	0.57	−0.23	−29
Bottom third of education	0.77	0.54	−0.23	−30

Source: Author's tabulations of CPS data.

necessary for some women (although some men and women might be more desirous of it). Sadly, social scientists have not yet been able to explain the changes in family structure. Research has not shown powerful effects of welfare, in part because benefits have been falling in real terms. Some have hypothesized that the changing fortunes of men and women may be playing a role, but the case is unproven.

One simple table illustrates both the limitations and the potential of using economic changes to understand changing family patterns (table 1.12). An examination of the marriage patterns of men between the ages of twenty-five and forty-four by level of education reveals a strong pattern. In 1973 (and in fact throughout the 1960s and early 1970s), the fraction of men who were married and living with their spouse hardly varied by level of education. Since that time marriage rates of all groups have declined, even those in the top education group, whose incomes have risen. Thus changing male fortunes cannot explain everything. But for the bottom two-thirds of men, where pay was stagnating, marriage declined much more than for the top third. And by 1996, there were dramatic differences in marriage by level of education. These data suggest that economic forces played a critical role in altering the formation of families, but we do not fully understand the reasons for the change in family structure.

Summarizing the American Economy

In this chapter, I have documented monumental changes in work, wages, families, and incomes. The focus was on getting the facts straight, not explaining their underlying causes. When economists have looked at whether technology or trade or immigration or a rising service economy or declining unionism or altered government policy or a failure of education to improve the quality of the workforce have been to blame, they have been able to answer, yes they have. All have contributed, often in complex and interactive ways. No one factor such as trade can explain very much, but somehow the growing power of technology and the increasingly competitive economic climate seem to be pushing toward declining rewards for less-skilled workers and greater pay for more-skilled workers (for a wonderful summary of what is known about the causes of the changes in pay, see Freeman 1997).

This chapter is concerned with what the changes have meant for workers and families. The American economy grew, and grew rather robustly, in the past quarter century. What was so unusual about this period was the wide divergence in the fortunes of different Americans. This rising tide certainly did not lift all boats the way that the growth of the 1960s did.

- The biggest winners in the recent quarter century were the well-to-do. Higher-paid workers (both men and women), owners of capital, and their children all gained significantly.

- Women's earnings rose dramatically at all levels. Roughly two-thirds of the rise was due to more hours of work or the higher pay associated with greater work experience. But some of the gap in pay between men and women closed.

- Men in the bottom two-thirds of the wage distribution gained little or nothing. In the lower wage groupings, wages were lower than they were twenty-three years ago. And median male wages were essentially stagnant for the entire time.

- The shifts in compensation strongly favored those with more skills and education. The gap in wages between those with more education and those with less widened dramatically.

- In families with two workers, the gains of women more than offset the losses of men on average, and incomes rose at least slightly as women worked more outside the home.

- But the changes in family structure and the fall in men's pay meant that incomes fell dramatically for children in the bottom third of families. For the bottom third of children, family income is 16 percent lower than it was almost a quarter century ago.

- In virtually every category and by every measure, the disparity in wages and incomes grew dramatically for both workers and families.

Recently—since 1996—there has been an upturn in wages. The wage distribution has narrowed slightly since workers at the bottom have improved relative to those in the middle. The economy remained strong through 1999. If the economy remains robust, there is at least some reason to hope that some of the trends in inequality can be slowed and even reversed, though the improvements to date have been modest. The pay of the least skilled workers remains no higher than it was thirty years ago. This chapter has concentrated on longer-term trends. Even with several more years of strong growth, however, these basic patterns will remain. The nation is very far away from where it stood in 1973. And if a recession were to hit, there is good reason to believe that the recent gains would be rapidly lost.

The really important question may be whether productivity will begin a new long-term period of relatively high growth. By virtually every available measure, productivity per worker grew far more slowly between 1973 and 1996 than it did in the prior decades. Much of the growth of the overall pie in those years was the result of more work, not higher output per worker. Without productivity growth, for the wages of some workers to rise, the wages of other must fall. The limited growth in productivity we did achieve went to gains in pay for women and higher wage men. Since 1996, productivity growth has accelerated again. If, by some miracle, the recent productivity jump indicates a new era of economic growth, there is hope that wages of workers even at the bottom may start rising again, although inequality may still grow. But the causes of the sudden rise in productivity are as obscure as the reasons for the long period of slowdown. If the country returns soon to the trends of the twenty-five years prior to 1996, wages overall will not rise much. And families will be forced to send more workers into the labor market to keep their incomes rising. Families with only one potential worker will be in a particularly precarious position. Thus productivity becomes a critical issue.

Our understanding of productivity is hampered by what I regard as almost scandalously poor data on the subject. When wages for some groups are changing relative to those for others, it is natural to ask about productivity. Perhaps low-skill workers really are not any more productive than they used to be. If so, the only hope for improving their wages is to improve their productivity. But if their productivity is rising, then all the benefits of that higher productivity seem to be going to other workers or to the firm's owners, and then a very different set of solutions might be proposed. If we are to get a serious understanding of what factors are causing the dramatic change in our economic picture, we will need to improve these data.

Thus the picture of winners and losers is fairly clear-cut. A few critical issues concerning data deserve to be highlighted:

- Inflation adjustment makes an important difference for some results because it affects the trends in income. But it does not affect the basic

conclusion that some trends were far more positive than others because inflation adjustments alter all trends the same.
- Productivity measures need to be improved if we are to understand what is influencing our economy.

Still, in spite of some data limitations, the basic findings here are quite robust. Returning to figure 1.1 and the seeming puzzle in the statistics, how the economy has performed depends not so much on what data one is using as on whom one is looking at in the data.

Appendix

Figure 1A.1   Ratio of Aggregate CPS Wage and Salary Income to NIPA Data, 1961 to 1995

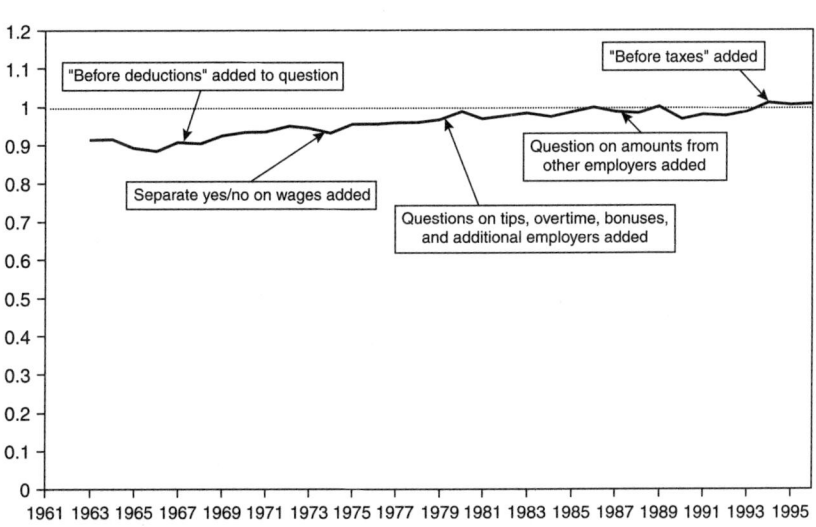

Source: Author's tabulations of NIPA data and March CPS data.

34 A Working Nation

Table 1A.1 Comparison of National Income per Adult and Median Earnings of Full-Year, Full-Time Male Workers Using Alternative Adjustments for Inflation, 1973 and 1996 (1996 U.S. Dollars Unless Otherwise Noted)

Indicator	1973	1996	Absolute Change	Percentage Change
Unadjusted nominal dollars				
National income per adult	8,050	31,981	23,931	297
Median earnings of full-year, full-time male workers	10,800	32,000	21,200	196
Ratio of national income per adult to median earnings	0.75	1.00		
Inflation adjusted to 1996 dollars using CPI-UX1				
National income per adult	26,759	31,981	5,222	20
Median earnings of full-year, full-time male workers	35,901	32,000	–3,901	–11
Ratio of national income per adult to median earnings	0.75	1.00		
Inflation adjusted to 1996 dollars using PCE				
National income per adult	26,450	31,981	5,531	21
Median earnings of full-year, full-time male workers	35,487	32,000	–3,487	–10
Ratio of national income per adult to median earnings	0.75	1.00		
Inflation adjusted to 1996 dollars using PCE less 0.5 percent				
National income per adult	23,707	31,981	8,274	35
Median earnings of full-year, full-time male workers	31,807	32,000	193	1
Ratio of national income per adult to median earnings	0.75	1.00		
Inflation adjusted to 1996 dollars using PCE less 1.0 percent				
National income per adult	21,237	31,981	10,744	51
Median earnings of full-year, full-time male workers	28,493	32,000	3,507	12
Ratio of national income per adult to median earnings	0.75	1.00		

Source: Author's calculations.
Note: Shaded area contains corrections used for tables in this chapter.

Table 1A.2 National Income per Adult and Components Adjusted by the CPI-U-X1, 1973 and 1996 (1996 U.S. Dollars Unless Otherwise Noted)

	1973	1996	Absolute Change	Percentage Change
Total national income per adult	26,754	31,981	5,227	20
Component				
Profits, rents, proprietors' income, and net interest	7,543	9,345	1,802	24
Total compensation for female wage and salary workers[a]				
Women with wages in top one-third	2,631	4,792	2,161	82
Women with wages in middle one-third	1,424	2,263	839	59
Women with wages in bottom one-third	533	904	372	70
Total compensation for male wage and salary workers[a]				
Men with wages in top one-third	8,055	9,127	1,072	13
Men with wages in middle one-third	4,654	3,985	−668	−14
Men with wages in bottom one-third	1,913	1,564	−348	−18

Source: Author's calculations of the CPS data.
Note: All figures are per adult age eighteen and over and adjusted by the CPI-U-X1.
[a] Includes employer-paid benefits and supplements and adjustments to make the CPS and NIPA data comparable.

Table 1A.3 Wages of Men Adjusted by the CPI-U-X1, 1973 and 1996 (1996 U.S. Dollars Unless Otherwise Noted)

Indicator	1973	1996	Absolute Change	Percentage Change
Fraction of adult men who worked at all during the year	0.77	0.73	−0.04	−5
Average hours worked per week by men who worked	37.6	38.5	0.9	2
Mean wage by wage thirds				
Men in the top one-third of wages	27.21	30.62	3.41	13

(*Table continues on p. 36.*)

Table 1A.3 *Continued*

Indicator	1973	1996	Absolute Change	Percentage Change
Men in the middle one-third of wages	14.41	12.93	−1.48	−10
Men in the bottom one-third of wages	7.61	6.45	−1.17	−15
Median wage by education				
More than college	21.80	24.23	2.43	11
College graduate	18.58	17.31	−1.27	−7
Some post–high school	14.44	12.50	−1.94	−13
High school graduate	14.29	11.54	−2.75	−19
Less than high school	11.74	7.93	−3.81	−32
Median wage by education				
Men age eighteen to twenty-four	9.02	6.97	−2.05	−23
Men age twenty-five to thirty-four	14.87	11.54	−3.33	−22
Men age thirty-five to forty-four	17.15	14.90	−2.25	−13
Men age forty-five to fifty-four	17.15	16.78	−0.37	−2
Men age fifty-five to sixty-four	15.15	15.32	−0.16	1
Median wage by race				
White men	14.44	12.98	−1.46	−10
African American men	10.32	10.55	0.23	2
Spanish ethnicity men	n.a.	8.50	n.a.	n.a.

Source: Author's calculations of the CPS data.
Note: All figures are per adult age eighteen and over and adjusted by the CPI-U-X1.
[a] Calculated using aggregate earnings divided by aggregate hours for the group.

Table 1A.4 Work and Wages of Men with Benefits Imputed and Correction for CPS Underreporting Adjusted by the CPI-U-X1, 1973 and 1996 (1996 U.S. Dollars Unless Otherwise Noted)

Indicator	1973	1996	Absolute Change	Percentage Change
Men in the top one-third of the wage distribution				
CPS wages	27.21	30.62	3.41	13
Imputed employer-paid benefits	3.95	6.41	2.46	62

Table 1A.4 *Continued*

Indicator	1973	1996	Absolute Change	Percentage Change
CPS correction to match NIPA	1.75	−0.15	−1.90	
Total hourly compensation	32.92	36.88	3.97	12
Men in the middle one-third of the wage distribution				
CPS wages	14.41	12.93	−1.48	−10
Imputed employer-paid benefits	2.48	3.04	0.57	23
CPS correction to match NIPA	0.93	−0.06	−0.99	
Total hourly compensation	17.81	15.91	−1.90	−11
Men in the bottom one-third of the wage distribution				
CPS wages	7.61	6.45	−1.17	−15
Imputed employer-paid benefits	1.12	1.21	0.09	8
CPS correction to match NIPA	0.49	−0.03	−0.52	
Total hourly compensation	9.23	7.63	−1.60	−17

Source: Published NIPA data and author's tabulations of CPS data.
Note: All figures are per adult age eighteen and over and adjusted by the CPI-U-X1.

Table 1A.5 Work and Wages of Women Adjusted by the CPI-U-X1, 1973 and 1996 (1996 U.S. Dollars Unless Otherwise Noted)

Indicator	1973	1996	Absolute Change	Percentage Change
Fraction of adult men who worked at all during the year	0.49	0.61	0.12	24
Average hours worked per week by women who worked	27.8	32.0	4.3	15
Mean wage by wage thirds				
Women in the top one-third of wages	15.54	20.68	5.14	33
Women in the middle one-third of wages	8.54	9.83	1.28	15
Women in the bottom one-third of wages	4.47	5.17	0.70	16
Median wage by education				
More than college	15.66	18.33	2.68	17
College graduate	11.85	13.46	1.61	14
Some post–high school	9.32	9.62	0.29	3

(Table continues on p. 38.)

Table 1A.5 *Continued*

Indicator	1973	1996	Absolute Change	Percentage Change
High school graduate	8.41	8.17	−0.24	−3
Less than high school	6.72	6.12	−0.60	−9
Median wage by race				
White women	8.61	9.61	1.00	12
African American women	6.42	8.63	2.21	34
Spanish ethnicity women	n.a.	7.50	n.a.	n.a.
Median wage by age				
All women age eighteen to twenty-four	7.10	6.15	−0.95	−13
All women age twenty-five to thirty-four	9.39	9.62	0.22	2
All women age thirty-five to forty-four	9.02	10.82	1.79	20
All women age forty-five to fifty-four	9.22	11.06	1.84	20
All women age fifty-five to sixty-four	8.87	9.94	1.07	12

Source: Published NIPA data and author's tabulations of CPS data.
Note: All figures are per adult age eighteen and over and adjusted by the CPI-U-X1.
[a] Calculated using aggregate earnings divided by aggregate hours for the group.

Table 1A.6 Work and Wages of Women with Benefits Imputed and Adjustments for CPS Underreporting of Men Adjusted by the CPI-U-X1, 1973 and 1996 (1996 U.S. Dollars Unless Otherwise Indicated)

Indicator	1973	1996	Absolute Change	Percentage Change
Women in the top one-third of the wage distribution				
CPS wages	15.54	20.68	5.14	33
Imputed employer-paid benefits	2.69	4.80	2.11	78
CPS correction to match NIPA	1.00	−0.10	−1.10	
Total hourly compensation	19.23	25.37	6.15	32
Women in the middle one-third of the wage distribution				
CPS wages	8.54	9.83	1.28	15
Imputed employer-paid benefits	1.36	2.20	0.84	62
CPS correction to match NIPA	0.55	−0.05	−0.60	
Total hourly compensation	10.45	11.98	1.53	15

Table 1A.6 *Continued*

Indicator	1973	1996	Absolute Change	Percentage Change
Women in the bottom one-third of the wage distribution				
CPS wages	4.47	5.17	0.70	16
Imputed employer-paid benefits	0.63	0.91	0.28	45
CPS correction to match NIPA	0.25	−0.03	−0.28	
Total hourly compensation	5.35	6.05	0.70	13

Source: Published NIPA data and author's tabulations of CPS data.
Note: All figures are for adult age eighteen and over and adjusted by the CPI-U-X1.

Table 1A.7 Work and Income for Two-Parent Families with Children by Education Grouping Adjusted by the CPI-U-X1, 1973 and 1996 (1996 U.S. Dollars Unless Otherwise Noted)

Indicator	1973	1996	Absolute Change	Percentage Change
Two-parent families in the top third of parental education[a]				
Husband's earnings	52,079	60,241	8,162	16
Wife's earnings	7,291	21,978	14,686	201
Other family income	4,335	6,409	2,074	48
Total family income	63,705	88,628	24,923	39
Average weekly work hours of husband	43	44	2	4
Average weekly work hours of wife	13	24	12	91
Mean number of children	2.1	1.9	−0.2	−12
Two-parent families in the middle third of parental education[a]				
Husband's earnings	38,341	35,399	−2,942	−8
Wife's earnings	6,073	13,895	7,822	129
Other family income	3,865	4,170	305	8
Total family income	48,279	53,463	5,184	11
Average weekly work hours of husband	42	42	0	0
Average weekly work hours of wife	14	24	11	78
Mean number of children	2.1	1.9	−0.2	−10

(Table continues on p. 40.)

Table 1A.7 *Continued*

Indicator	1973	1996	Absolute Change	Percentage Change
Two-parent families in the bottom third of parental education[a]				
Husband's earnings	28,820	25,620	−3,200	−11
Wife's earnings	4,792	9,942	5,150	107
Other family income	5,929	4,326	−1,602	−27
Total family income	39,541	39,889	348	1
Average weekly work hours of husband	38	38	0	−1
Average weekly work hours of wife	12	20	8	64
Mean number of children	2.4	2.0	−0.4	−15

Source: Author's tabulations of the CPS data.
[a] Calculated based on parental income for both two-parent and single-parent families.

Table 1A.8 Work and Income for Single-Parent Families with Children by Education Grouping Adjusted by the CPI-U-X1, 1973 and 1996 (1996 U.S. Dollars Unless Otherwise Noted)

Indicator	1973	1996	Absolute Change	Percentage Change
Single-parent families in the top third of parental education[a]				
Head's earnings	19,607	31,917	12,310	63
Other family income	11,699	7,484	−4,215	−36
Total family income	31,306	39,401	8,095	26
Average weekly work hours of head	27	36	9	32
Mean number of children	1.8	1.6	−0.2	−12
Single-parent families in the middle third of parental education[a]				
Head's earnings	13,021	16,738	3,717	29
Other family income	9,572	5,076	−4,496	−47
Total family income	22,593	21,814	−779	−3
Average weekly work hours of head	23	29	5	22
Mean number of children	2.1	1.7	−0.4	−19

Table 1A.8 *Continued*

Indicator	1973	1996	Absolute Change	Percentage Change
Single-parent families in the bottom third of parental education[a]				
Head's earnings	6,438	10,679	4,241	66
Other family income	10,737	5,205	−5,532	−52
Total family income	17,175	15,884	−1,291	−8
Average weekly work hours of head	14	22	7	52
Mean number of children	2.4	1.9	−0.6	−24

Source: Author's tabulations of the CPS data.
[a] Calculated based on parental income for both two-parent and single-parent families.

Table 1A.9 Family Income and Family Structure for Children by Family Income Groups Adjusted by the CPI-U-X1, 1973 and 1996 (1996 U.S. Dollars Unless Otherwise Noted)

Indicator	1973	1996	Absolute Change	Percentage Change
Children with family income in the top third				
Average family income	78,771	99,855	21,084	27
Fraction of children in two-parent families	0.98	0.96	−0.01	−1
Children with family income in the middle third				
Average family income	41,381	40,053	−1,328	−3
Fraction of children in two-parent families	0.94	0.84	−0.10	−11
Children with family income in the bottom third				
Average family income	18,819	13,987	−4,832	−26
Fraction of children in two-parent families	0.62	0.43	−0.19	−31

Source: Author's tabulations of the CPS data.

Chapter 2

The New Employee-Employer Relationship

Have the connections between employers and employees in the United States weakened in recent years? Substantial popular attention has been paid to downsizing, the growth of the temporary workforce, and other trends that seem to signal a general decline in job security and company loyalty among American workers. Are we in fact seeing a basic change in the employee-employer relationship in the United States in which workers are being treated more as disposable factors of production who can be easily replaced by technology or overseas production? What workplace policies or practices hold promise for creating win-win situations—enhancing business performance along with employment security and compensation of American workers? What potential does rewarding employees based on business performance—through profit sharing, employee ownership, or gain-sharing plans—have for improving the employer-employee relationship and economic performance?

This chapter reviews available evidence, contributes new evidence on these questions, and discusses government policies to improve workplace relations and performance. First, a broad range of labor market evidence is used to assess trends in the employee-employer relationship, including worker displacement and long-term employment relationships, contingent work, worker training, and employee attitudes.

The chapter then examines how work is organized in the United States, focusing on a variety of workplace practices—employee involvement, training, contingent pay, and others—that can enhance performance. Employee participation in ownership and profits has often been seen as a way to increase workplace cooperation and business performance; in addition, employee ownership has been promoted for broadening the distribution of wealth, and profit sharing has been promoted for increasing employment stability. We review these subjects using a variety of evidence.

Finally, we contrast two paths for employee-employer relationships in the next twenty years: one path with further weakening of employee-employer connections where workers are seen as a variable cost with substantial job insecurity and the other path with stronger connections and higher workplace performance based on extensive training and greater employee participation in decisions, ownership, and profits. This second path might be labeled shared capitalism—encouraging more widespread participation in economic decisions and rewards and working against a division of society into the haves and have-nots.[1] To stimulate discussion on the second path, we present several policy initiatives designed to combat problems of information and inertia and to encourage practices that can have larger societal benefits.

Evidence on Trends in Employee-Employer Relationships

A basic element of the employee-employer relationship is its expected longevity. Jobs can be ended by employers through layoffs, plant closings, or individual firings or by employees through quits and retirements. Particular concern has been paid in the past fifteen years to worker displacement through layoffs and plant closings, often linked to international competition, deregulation, technological change, and general corporate restructuring. Since firms can often deal with outside pressures in a number of ways, the choice to lay off workers can signal decreased commitment by employers to their current employees. Whether within the firm's control or not, as the prospect of displacement grows, both employees and employers are less likely to invest in and be committed to the current employment relationship (although employees may display more commitment if they perceive that doing so will increase their chances of being retained). Similarly, higher quit rates among employees may signal decreased commitment to employers, and higher prospects of quitting will lead both employers and employees to invest less in the current relationship. Given the importance of the expected longevity of the employment relationship, this section starts with a review of worker displacement and job tenure data, before moving on to other indicators of how employee-employer relationships may have been changing.

Worker Displacement Rates and Trends

Figure 2.1 provides trends from 1981 to 1995 in displacement rates for all workers and for those who had been with their employers for at least three years (Farber 1997b, 1998, 2000; Hipple 1999).[2] Overall, the risk of a worker being displaced in a three-year period fluctuated between

Figure 2.1 Trends in Worker Displacement Rates

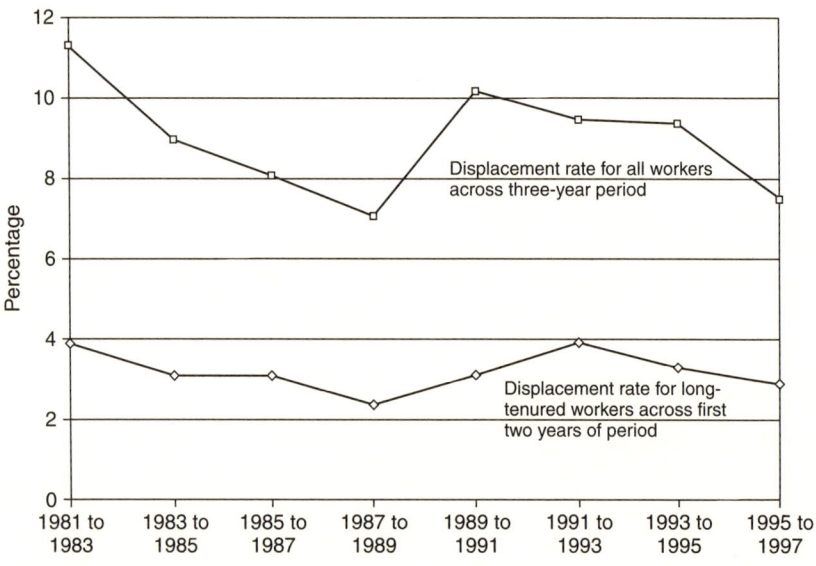

Source: Farber 2000; Hipple 1999.

about 8 percent and 11 percent. Displacement rates clearly varied with the business cycle, being highest in the recession years from 1981 to 1983 and from 1989 to 1991. Controlling for cyclicality, there appears to have been a secular increase in the displacement rate, since the displacement rates in the mid-1990s were not very different from those in the early 1980s when the economy was less strong and unemployment rates were higher (Farber 1998, 10; 2000, 19).

This finding is supported by recent studies using other methods and data sets and by data on employee attitudes indicating a general increase in the percentage of workers believing they are likely to lose their job in the next year, which appears to be a factor in moderating wage increases.[3]

Displacement risks are not equal across workers. Figures 2.2 and 2.3 provide breakdowns of displacement risk by broad occupation, showing the following:

- Displacement risks are clearly higher for those in blue-collar occupations (craftspersons, operatives, and laborers), whose particularly high risk of job loss in recession periods indicates that they bear the brunt of cyclical downturns.

Figure 2.2 Displacement Rates Among All Workers, by Occupation

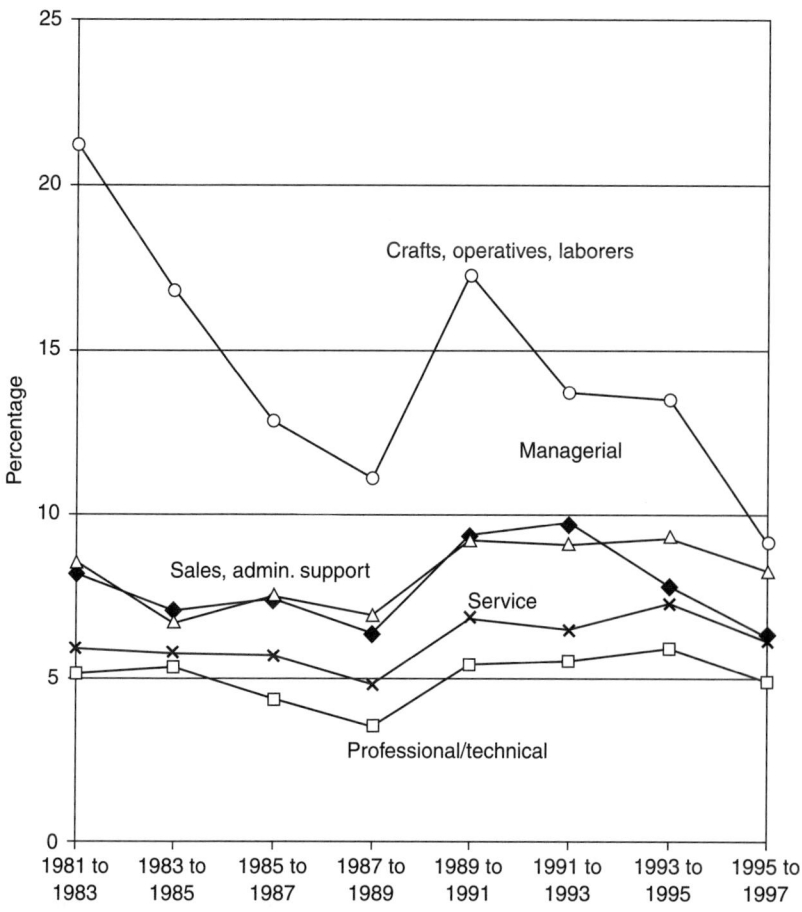

Source: Farber 2000.

- Although the displacement risk for blue-collar workers has fallen since the early 1980s, the risk for other workers remained stable or rose through the 1990s.
- Therefore, while blue-collar workers remain at higher risk of displacement, any secular increase in job loss appears to be concentrated in white-collar and service occupations.
- Consistent with these findings, displacement rates have almost doubled in the largely white-collar industries of professional

Figure 2.3 Displacement Rates Among Long-Tenured Workers by Occupation, 1981 to 1997

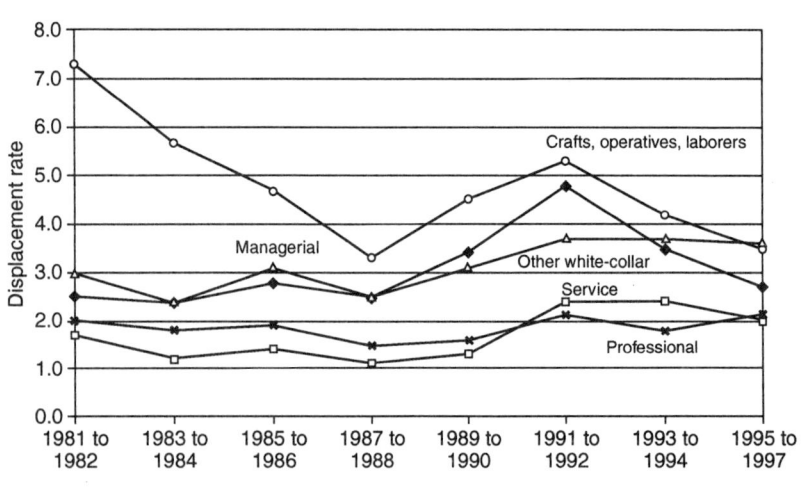

Source: Hipple 1999.

services and finance, insurance, and real estate, while rates in other industries generally have not increased (Farber 2000, 75–76).

Analysis of demographic characteristics shows the following:

- While African American men did have higher displacement rates than white men in the early 1980s (largely because black men are disproportionately likely to be in blue-collar jobs), the displacement rates for black and white men have converged since that time due to increased displacement among white-collar jobs (Fairlie and Kletzer 1996).
- The displacement rates for men with high school or less education are higher than for women and college graduates, but they did not increase during this time period; the rates did increase for female high school graduates and for both male and female college graduates (Farber 1997a, 67–68).

Costs of Worker Displacement

Displacement would not be a major concern if workers were able to obtain similar jobs fairly quickly. Unfortunately, many workers endure long spells before being reemployed, and many obtain significantly lower earnings in their future employment:

- Between three-fifths and three-fourths (58 to 77 percent) of workers displaced in a three-year period have jobs at the end of the period, while slightly more workers displaced from long-tenure jobs (75 to 83 percent) have jobs more than a year following displacement (Farber 2000, 37; Hipple 1999, 21).
- Reemployment is particularly slow for women, nonwhites, and individuals without a college degree.[4]
- Displacement often strongly affects subsequent earnings. For long-tenure workers who were displaced in the early 1990s (1991 to 1994), those reemployed in full-time jobs more than a year later had an average 15 percent decline in weekly earnings, although the average decline was only 4 percent among those displaced in the strong growth years of 1995 to 1996 who had a full-time job in 1998. There are greater earnings losses on average among older workers, blacks, and individuals with no college education (Hipple 1999, 27). Earnings losses are not made up after several years: Louis S. Jacobson, Robert J. LaLonde, and Daniel G. Sullivan (1993) found quarterly earnings losses averaging $2,000 for workers displaced four years ago, while Stevens (1997) found annual earnings losses averaging 9 percent for workers displaced more than six years ago (due both to reduced hourly wages and to reduced hours of work).[5] A substantial portion of the lost earnings reflects the lost value of skills that were not transferable to other firms or industries (reviewed in Kletzer 1998, 127–30).
- The costs of displacement are higher during recessions when fewer jobs are available, but there is no evidence that displacement costs have grown systematically over time (Farber 2000, 65–66).

Reasons for Worker Displacement

What is behind the apparent increase in the rate of job loss in recent years? One important factor in worker displacement is international trade. Robert Haveman (1994, cited in Kletzer 1998) estimates that a 1 percent decline in industry import prices is linked to a 1.62 percent increase in worker displacement in an industry, with the relationship twice as strong among import-sensitive industries such as apparel, footwear, and textiles. Not only does growth in imports appear to increase displacement rates (while growth in exports decreases displacement rates), but also general trade sensitivity (high levels of import and export penetration) is linked

48   A Working Nation

to higher displacement rates, possibly because trade-sensitive industries are exposed to international as well as domestic supply and demand shocks (Addison, Fox, and Ruhm 1995).

Apart from international trade, can displacement be linked to corporate restructuring, downsizing, technological change, or other factors? Although limited systematic evidence is available here, some insights can be gained by examining the types of displacement identified by employees and the reasons for mass layoffs identified by employers. Employee-reported data indicate the following:

- There has been a slight decline since the early 1980s in displacements due to plant closings (Farber 2000, 68).

- The rate of job loss due to the abolition of one's position or shift has increased since 1990, which may reflect an increase in corporate restructuring and downsizing not linked to decreases in product demand (Farber 1998).[6]

More direct evidence is available from employers who were asked about the reasons for mass layoffs. In 1996 and 1997 there were more than 11,000 mass layoffs in which at least fifty workers were laid off for at least thirty days, involving a total of 2.2 million workers.[7] Table 2.1 presents data on mass layoffs broken down by employer-reported reasons showing the following:

- The most common reasons given for such layoffs are seasonal work, contract completion, and slack work, which generally are not under the control of the company.

- Among reasons that generally are under the employer's control, company reorganizations accounted for about 194,000 layoffs, and changes in business ownership accounted for about 69,000 layoffs in 1996 and 1997.

- International trade is a relatively minor factor in mass layoffs, with about 26,000 layoffs due to import competition and 15,000 layoffs due to overseas relocation in 1996 and 1997.

- Employers directly identified automation as responsible for less than 8,000 layoffs, although technological change may be a factor behind other reasons, particularly reorganizations and domestic relocations.

- There has been no apparent increase since 1986 in the share of layoffs due to change in business ownership, domestic relocation, import competition, or overseas relocation, but there have been more layoffs due to corporate reorganizations and automation.[8]

Table 2.1 Reasons for Extended Mass Layoffs, Various Years, 1986 to 1997

	Number of Workers Laid Off, 1996 to 1997			Percentage Breakdowns Over Time, Excluding Seasonal Work[a]			
Reason	1996 (1)	1997 (2)	Total (3)	1986 to 1987 (4)	1988 to 1989 (5)	1990 to 1991 (6)	1996 to 1997 (7)
Total workers laid off[a]	1,158,199	1,103,046	2,261,245	527,161	702,378	989,321	1,273,516
Number of states reporting[a]	50	50	50	13–29	42–44	45–48	50
Seasonal work	488,398	499,331	987,729				
Contract completed	124,506	175,572	300,078	11.9	14.5	6.6	23.6
Slack work	112,313	90,382	202,695	32.1	24.5	34.9	15.9
Reorganization within company	115,669	78,324	193,993	NR	NR	NR	15.2
Bankruptcy	21,247	21,537	42,784	2.3	5.0	8.0	3.4
Financial difficulty	56,749	39,634	96,383	NR	NR	NR	7.6
Business ownership change	43,425	25,141	68,566	5.9	5.4	3.5	5.4
Labor dispute	14,119	16,149	30,268	3.3	6.2	NR	2.4
Domestic relocation	11,323	15,241	26,564	2.5	3.4	4.4	2.1
Import competition	13,684	12,493	26,177	2.6	2.4	2.0	2.1
Overseas relocation	4,326	10,435	14,761	3.4	0.3	0.6	1.2
Automation	5,522	2,117	7,639	0.2	0.3	0.6	0.6
Other[b]	124,703	94,506	219,209	26.9	23.8	29.5	17.2
Not reported	22,215	22,184	44,399	8.9	14.1	7.3	3.5

Source: Based on data provided by Pat Carey, local area unemployment statistics program of the Bureau of Labor Statistics.
Note: Extended mass layoff events are defined as fifty or more initial claims for unemployment insurance benefits over a five week period, with at least fifty workers separated for more than thirty days.
NR: Not reported.

[a] The reporting program in the period 1986 to 1991 did not cover all states (never including California), so the breakdowns in columns four to six may not represent national patterns. Also, corporate reorganization and financial difficulty were not included as possible reasons during this time. Therefore, the comparisons across years are only suggestive of trends and should be interpreted with caution. In the second row, the first (second) number represents the number of states reporting data for the first (second) given year in columns four to six.
[b] Other reasons given, in order of importance in 1996 to 1997, were contract cancellation, vacation period, weather-related, product line discontinued, model changeover, plant or machine repair, material shortage, and natural disaster.

Long-Term Employment Relationships

Trends in employee tenure with an employer provide another way to examine the issue of job stability and security. If employers have been more likely to lay off workers or workers have been more likely to move between employers, then average levels of employee tenure with an employer will have declined. (It is possible, though, for layoffs and general job insecurity to increase without a change in observed levels of tenure, if quit rates decrease as employees hang on to their current jobs in an insecure environment.)

Figures 2.4 and 2.5 look at trends in long-term employment relationships (based on data from Farber 1997c):

- Long-tenure jobs have apparently decreased among men, but not among women. The percentage of thirty-five- to sixty-four-year-old males in jobs with more than ten years tenure has declined from 50 to 40 percent since 1979, while the figure for women has stayed fairly constant around 30 percent. A similar pattern is evident in jobs with more than twenty years tenure, where the male percentage has declined from 34 to 27 percent, while the female percentage has risen slightly from 13 to 14 percent. Only a small portion of this overall decline for men can be accounted for by changes in demographic, occupational, or industry composition.[9]

- This pattern is also reflected in a decline from 1983 to 1996 from 5.9 to 5.3 median years of tenure for men in wage and salary jobs who are age twenty-five or older, compared with a constant 5.0 median years of tenure for women (even though one would expect median tenure to decline as more women join the labor force; Bureau of Labor Statistics 1997b). The decline in median years of tenure was strongest among older men, helping to explain the growth of anxiety about job security because older persons have stronger expectations of sustained tenure.[10] Henry S. Farber (1997c) investigated the possibility that employers have been targeting long-tenure men for layoff, but long-tenure men did not make up a greater share of job losers over this time.

- Decreases in average tenure have occurred in most broad occupations. Although blue-collar workers are unique among the major occupations in having declining displacement rates, they follow other major occupations in decreases in tenure. As shown in figure 2.5, the percentage of workers with more than twenty years of tenure has declined among all broad occupations except for clerical and service workers. These findings of decreased job stability also apply to jobs of more than ten years and are consistent with other recent research.[11]

Figure 2.4 Trends in Long-Term Employment Relationships by Age and Gender, 1979 to 1996

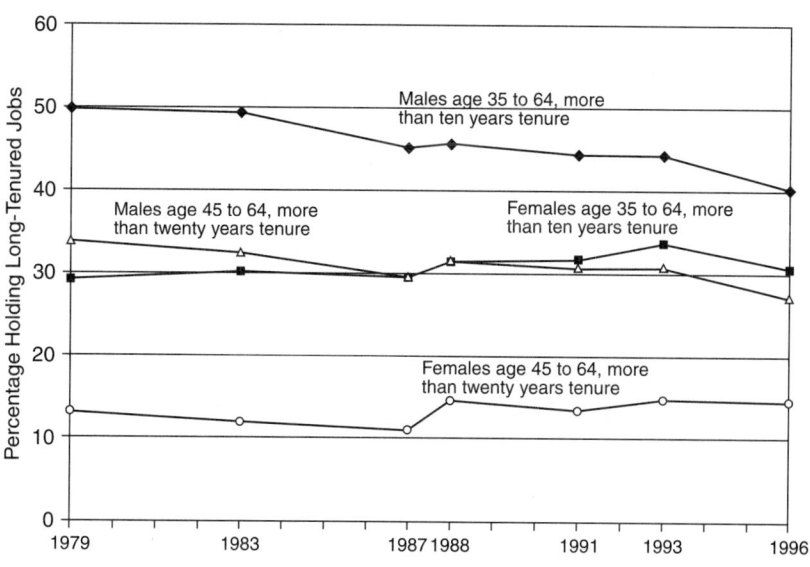

Source: Farber 1997c.

Figure 2.5 Long-Term Employment Relationships by Occupation, 1979 to 1996

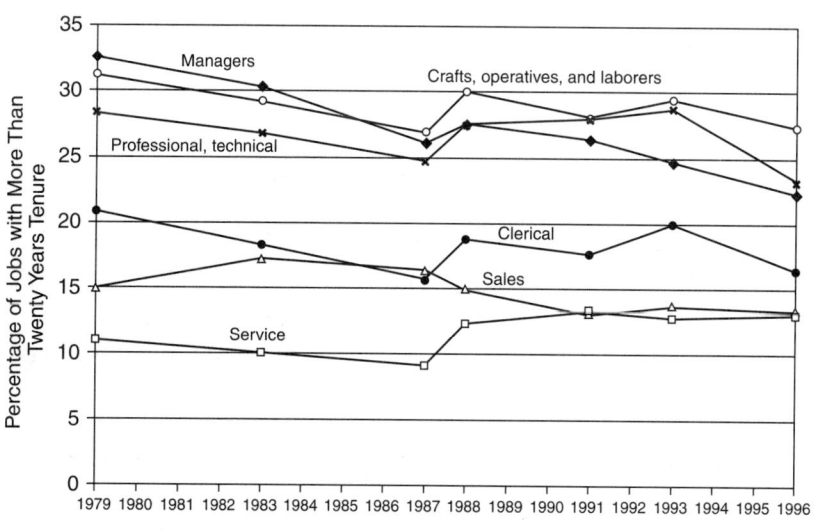

Source: Farber 1997c.

In summary, there is evidence of decreased job security and stability. There appears to have been a secular increase in displacement risks since 1980, particularly for white-collar and service workers, and a decline of long-term employment relationships among men, although not among women. Given the substantial costs often associated with displacement, more attention is being paid to the need for employees to develop broad skills applicable in many settings, enhancing their mobility and overall career rather than their prospects at a single employer (Arthur and Rousseau 1996).

Contingent Employment

Contingent work, which may take a variety of forms, has received increased attention over the past decade. Discussions of job insecurity often highlight the growth of the temporary help industry, in which workers sign up with agencies contracting with and assigning workers to firms needing work done, but not wanting to hire long-term employees at that point. Many workers desire such jobs, which give them the flexibility and the chance to sample different employers without committing to a long-term relationship, but many of these workers say that they would prefer a more stable employment arrangement. Various other types of workers also are referred to as contingent workers with little or no job security, including on-call and day laborers, many self-employed independent contractors and part-time workers, and individuals holding regular wage and salary jobs that have a substantial risk of disappearing. Although one of the principal problems of contingent work is uncertainty in employment and earnings, other problems can be lower earnings and access to benefits and reductions in worker voice and influence in the workplace (Blank 1998, 261–62).

Research on the temporary help services industry shows the following:

- Employment in this industry grew from 0.5 percent of all employment in 1982 to almost 2.0 percent in 1996 (Blank 1998, 272).[12]
- Just over one-third of temporary employees work in clerical occupations, and one-third work in blue-collar occupations (Blank 1998, 272).
- Temporary employees are disproportionately likely to be female, young, and from poor families and to not have a college degree.[13]
- The average hourly pay is $7.24, less than two-thirds the average hourly pay of $11.24 for other full-time workers, and temporary workers are less likely to receive health insurance, pensions, and

other benefits through work (Hipple and Stewart 1996; Blank 1998, 266–67).

Other types of contingent workers include independent contractors, on-call and day laborers, and workers in contract firms who generally have short-term employment situations. As shown in table 2.2, such workers together with temporary help agency workers constitute close to one-tenth of the workforce (Nardone, Veum, and Yates 1997; Cohany 1998). It is noteworthy, however, that independent contractors earn more than workers in traditional jobs (columns five to six), and less than one-tenth say they would prefer a traditional job compared with half or more of on-call and day laborers and temporary help agency workers (column seven).

Since the definition of contingent worker is open to debate, the Bureau of Labor Statistics has developed three measures of the contingent workforce. Findings from the 1995 and 1997 surveys, as presented in table 2.2, show the following:

- Contingent workers number between 2.4 million and 5.6 million (using the most and least restrictive definitions), representing 1.9 to 4.4 percent of the workforce.
- Average pay is 20 to 30 percent lower for contingent workers under each of the definitions.
- More than half (55 to 60 percent) of contingent workers say they would prefer noncontingent employment.[14]
- Each of the three measures shows a declining rate of contingent employment from 1995 to 1997, indicating an increase in job security as unemployment rates dropped and the labor market tightened (Bureau of Labor Statistics 1998).

The past several decades have also seen an increase in part-time employment, which has raised concern among many observers since many part-timers would prefer full-time jobs, and part-time jobs (like temporary help service jobs) tend to pay less, have less access to benefits, and have less job security than regular full-time jobs. Over the 1968 to 1996 period, the share of part-time workers increased among men (from 8 to 12 percent of all male workers) but generally did not increase among women (fluctuating between 26 and 30 percent of all female workers; Blank 1998, 265). Although most part-time work is voluntary—the worker prefers a part-time schedule—between 1968 and 1996 the share of involuntary part-time workers (preferring full-time work but not able to obtain it) increased from 15 to 22 percent of all women part-timers and

Table 2.2 Alternative and Contingent Employment, 1995 and 1997

	Employees in Alternative and Contingent Employment				Median Weekly Earnings as a Percentage of Traditional or Noncontingent Earnings, 1997		Percentage Preferring Traditional or Noncontingent Employment, 1997
	1995		1997				
Type of Worker	Thousands (1)	Percentage (2)	Thousands (3)	Percentage (4)	Full-time (5)	Part-time (6)	(7)
Total employed	123,208	100.0	126,742	100.0			
Independent contractors	8,309	6.7	8,456	6.7	102.5	131.3	9.3
On-call and day laborers	2,078	1.7	1,996	1.6	84.7	82.6	50.0
Temporary help agency workers	1,181	1.0	1,300	1.0	64.5	102.8	59.2
Workers provided by contract firms	652	0.5	809	0.6	121.4	100.7	
Subtotal	12,220	9.9	12,561	9.9			
Contingent worker estimates							
1. Wage or salary workers who worked in job less than one year and expect job to last less than one year[a]		2.2	2,739	1.9	69.8	69.9	60.2
2. (1) plus self-employed and independent contractors meeting same condition[a]		2.8	3,422	2.4	72.2	71.9	56.7
3. (2) including all wage or salary workers expecting job to last for limited time		4.9	6,034	4.4	81.8	76.0	55.5

Source: Cohany 1998; Hipple 1998; Nardone, Veum, and Yates 1997.
[a] Job duration for temporary help agency workers is determined with the agency for estimate 1 and with the client for estimate 2.

from one-fourth to one-third of all male part-timers (although it appeared to peak in the mid-1980s and has declined somewhat since then). Like temporary help service workers, part-timers are disproportionately young, female, and less educated.

Rebecca M. Blank (1998) provides alternative estimates of total and "problem" contingent workers. She combines all part-time workers with temporary help service workers and independent contractors to estimate that 22 percent of the workforce is in some sort of contingent job—a percentage that did not change appreciably between 1985 and 1995. Problem contingent employment is based on contingent workers who would prefer other employment arrangements.[15] As seen in table 2.3, between 4.6 and 8.5 percent of workers are in problem contingent jobs where other arrangements are preferred, with a slightly higher rate among workers with no more than a high school degree.[16]

The number of problem contingent workers decreased between 1985 and 1995, as the decline in the percentage involuntarily working part-time swamped the increases in temporary help workers and independent contractors desiring other arrangements.

Although firms' growing use of temporary help workers is clearly a phenomenon worthy of continued attention and study, these numbers indicate that contingent workers desiring other arrangements are not a growing problem in the U.S. labor market. (For further analysis and discussion of contingent work, see Barker and Christensen 1998.)

Training

Employee skills have become a more important factor in workplace productivity and worker earnings in the past twenty-five years. This is indicated in part by the rising earnings premium for education: young male college graduates in 1974 earned only 16 percent more than young male high school graduates, but in 1995 they earned 56 percent more.[17] Although technological change can sometimes have a deskilling effect, most employers report a rise in the skills required to perform jobs.[18] In addition, the rise in the earnings premium attached to computer use along with other evidence indicate that the overall effect of technological change in the past two decades has been to increase the skills required of employees (Krueger 1993; Cappelli 1993). More than ever, employees continually need to learn new skills following the end of their formal education. Research clearly supports the idea that training generally enhances workplace productivity as well as worker earnings (reviewed in Lynch 1994; Department of Labor 1995).

Apart from training's direct effect on a worker's ability to do a job, training can play an important role in the employee-employer rela-

Table 2.3 Prevalence of "Problem" Contingent Work, 1985 and 1995

Type of "Problem" Contingent Worker	1985		1995	
	Total Employed (Thousands)	Percentage of All Employed	Total Employed (Thousands)	Percentage of All Employed
Temporary help workers	284–476	0.3–0.4	405–678	0.3–0.5
Contract workers	602–803	0.6–0.7	806–1,075	0.6–0.9
Part-time workers	4,824–8,499	4.4–7.8	4,489–8,813	3.6–7.1
Total "problem" contingent workers preferring other arrangements	5,710–9,778	5.3–9.0	5,700–10,566	4.6–8.5
"Problem" contingent workers with no more than a high school degree	4,137–6,393	6.7–10.4	3,213–5,298	5.8–9.6

Source: Blank 1998.

tionship. Investments in training can often signal that one or both parties want and expect the employment relationship to continue. This is particularly true for investments in firm-specific training, where the skills learned are not readily transferable to other firms, giving both sides an incentive to maintain the relationship. It may also be true for investments in general training, such as training obtained through college tuition reimbursement, which may be financed by employers hoping to increase employee loyalty as well as skills. Workers are, in fact, less likely to experience unemployment following workplace training (Lillard and Tan 1992).[19]

The growing importance of skills in the modern workplace has led to much concern that worker skills are not keeping up, widening the gap between required and available skills. Although there are reasonably good measures of levels and changes in formal education over time (with an extensive literature documenting its effects), there are almost no consistent and representative measures across time on formal or informal worker training.

Trends during the 1980s come from employee reports of training in current population survey special supplements in 1983 and 1991 (from Bowers and Swaim 1994). These employee reports, summarized in table 2.4, indicate the following:

Table 2.4 Training Reported by Employees, 1983 and 1991 (Percentage)

Indicator	Any training		Schooling		Formal Company Training		Informal Training	
	1983 (1)	1991 (2)	1983 (3)	1991 (4)	1983 (5)	1991 (6)	1983 (7)	1991 (8)
Training needed for current job	55.4	55.8	29.5	32.1	9.6	12.1	27.9	27.1
Had skill-improvement training in current job								
All	36.4	41.7	12.1	13.1	12.0	16.8	15.2	16.2
By whether training needed for job								
Yes	46.9	55.2	18.7	20.1	16.3	23.3	15.7	18.8
No	23.3	24.3	4.0	4.3	6.6	8.5	14.4	12.8
By education								
No high school degree	17.3	18.4	2.2	2.2	3.8	5.2	11.7	10.8
High school degree	31.5	34.7	6.8	7.4	10.5	13.9	15.9	15.6
Some college	42.6	47.3	14.9	15.3	15.1	20.4	17.2	18.9
Four years of college	52.0	58.2	21.2	20.9	20.5	26.1	16.7	18.7
Five plus years of college	62.5	68.2	38.2	24.6	16.7	23.4	12.6	16.8

Source: Current Population Survey supplements, reported in Bowers and Swaim 1994.

58   A Working Nation

- There was little change in the schooling and training that workers thought were necessary to obtain their job over the 1983 to 1991 period.
- There was, however, a modest increase in the amount of skill-improvement training received while in their current job. The percentage of workers reporting some form of skill-improvement training in their current job rose from 36 to 42 percent, with the largest increase in formal company training (12 to 17 percent).

Increases in training were greater among those reporting that schooling or training was required to obtain their job and among those with higher levels of education. The greater amount of training accorded to workers who already had higher qualifications played a part in the widening of earnings inequality in the past twenty years.[20]

The prevalence of employee formal training may have increased since 1991, according to some employer-based evidence from the 1994 and 1997 national employer surveys. In the 1994 survey, almost three-fourths (72 percent) of establishments reported increasing their overall level of formal training over the period from 1991 to 1994, although the percentage of firms providing formal training appears to have declined slightly between 1994 and 1997.

How much employee training is currently being done? A more thorough assessment of the amount and types of training was done in the 1995 survey of employer-provided training, which collected results from both employers and employees in establishments with fifty or more employees (Frazis et al. 1998). The data presented in table 2.5 show the following:

- More than four-fifths of employees have received formal training with their current employer, while more than two-thirds have received it in the past twelve months.
- Over a six-month period in 1995, the average employee received just over ten hours of formal training (10.7 by employer reports and 13.4 by employee reports) and thirty-one hours of informal training.
- The most common types of formal training concern occupational safety, communications and quality, and computers, while the greatest number of formal training hours in 1995 was spent on computer training.
- Informal training is most common for production and construction work, which account for more than one-fourth of the total hours of informal training.
- Over a six-month period, an average $945 was spent on training per employee, with about two-thirds ($647) accounted for by wages and

salaries paid to employees during training and the next greatest expense ($139) accounted for by wages and salaries paid to in-house trainers.

Who is receiving the training? Table 2.6 shows that training is most prevalent in establishments that are large and have relatively low turnover and among employees who are full-time, college educated, high earners, long-tenure, and professional or technical workers. The new skills often needed by new employees are generally developed through informal training, which accounts for almost seven-eighths of the total training hours among employees with less than two years of tenure. Formal training is more likely to be provided to long-tenure employees, indicating that it is more likely when employers and employees are more committed to each other and the relationship appears to be a long-term one.

Is enough training taking place? This is an open question. Although skills gained on the job have become more important in recent years, U.S. workers receive less formal training in the workplace than do their European or Japanese counterparts (Lynch 1994, 75). Several features of the U.S. employment system may cause employers and employees to underinvest in training. Employers generally are unwilling to invest in worker training when they are unlikely to gain returns on the investment, such as when there is a significant risk of displacement or voluntary turnover. Training may even increase the likelihood of turnover, if the new skills are visible to other firms and make the employee attractive for "poaching" by other employers. Workers may not be able to borrow money to finance general skills training (possibly due to lack of collateral) and may not want to accept lower wages for training without a promise of employment security (since some skills may be specific to a firm, and it may be difficult to certify the general skills to other employers). U.S. workers do not appear to enjoy any earnings premium for training received on previous jobs, indicating that the skills learned were specific to the previous employer or that there was an information problem in certifying general skills to the new employer (Lynch 1992, 1994).

Training may be enhanced by a national certification system for skills gained through training (such as in Germany), employment guarantees with high costs to employee turnover (such as in Japan, which has lower turnover rates than other Western economies), sanctions against poaching trained employees (such as in Germany through chambers of commerce), or a tax system that encourages training (such as in France or Australia to help equalize the private and social rates of return on training; Lynch 1994, 65–70). The lack of such features in the United States, plus the growing displacement rates and decreased job stability for many workers, raises the concern that training levels may be insufficient.

Table 2.5 Types, Hours, and Costs of Training, 1995

Type of Training	Percentage Receiving Formal Training		Hours of Training per Employee, May to October, 1995			
	With Current Employer, Employee Survey (1)	In Past Twelve Months, Employee Survey (2)	Formal		Informal, Employee Survey (5)	Total, Employee Survey (6)
			Employer Survey (3)	Employee Survey (4)		
Any training	84.4	69.8	10.7	13.4	31.1	44.5
Type of training						
Job skills						
Management training	28.4	16.3	0.8	0.6	1.1	1.7
Professional and technical training	30.9	21.4	1.3	1.9	4.3	6.2
Computer training	38.4	23.5	2.1	5.1	6.8	11.8
Clerical and administrative training	18.7	8.4	0.5	0.6	2.8	3.4
Sales and customer relations training	26.6	15.1	0.8	0.6	2.6	3.2
Service related training	12.5	5.9	0.6	0.3	1.8	2.1
Production and construction training	21.0	11.3	1.1	2.0	8.6	10.6

General skills	6.7	2.3	0.1	0.0	0.3
Basic skills training					
Occupational safety training	58.0	42.8	1.2	0.6	2.4
Employee health and wellness training			0.2		
Orientation training			0.6		
Awareness training			0.1		
Communications and quality training	40.2	22.8	1.4	1.5	2.6
Other types of training	3.4	1.4	0.1	0.2	0.0
Training cost per employee (U.S. dollars)					
Wages and salaries of employees			138.5	224.1	422.8
Wages and salaries of in-house trainers			50.6		
Tuition reimbursements			97.7		
Payments to outside trainers			11.5		646.9
Contributions to training funds					

Source: Columns one to two and four to six are based on the survey of employees, and column three is based on the survey of employers, from the 1995 survey of employer-provided training (BLS 1996a, 1996b).

A Working Nation

Table 2.6 Training Prevalence and Hours by Trainee Characteristics, 1995

	Percentage who Received Training		Hours of Training per Employee, May to October 1995		
	With Current Employer	In Past Twelve Months	Formal	Informal	Total
Characteristic	(1)	(2)	(3)	(4)	(5)
All employees	84.4	69.8	13.4	31.1	44.5
Establishment size					
50 to 99 employees	78.9	61.6	8.2	31.9	40.1
100 to 499 employees	84.7	73.0	13.5	34.5	48.0
500+ employees	87.7	71.0	16.6	26.0	42.6
Establishment turnover rate[a]					
Low	87.4	78.0	27.3	19.0	46.3
Medium	89.8	74.7	15.6	30.4	46.0
High	75.5	60.7	7.6	34.2	41.8
Full-time employees	86.6	71.6	14.6	34.2	48.8
Part-time employees	68.5	56.1	4.8	7.7	12.5
Education					
High school or less	82.3	60.1	10.9	24.8	35.7
Some college	79.1	67.8	14.3	37.0	51.3
Bachelor's or higher	96.8	89.7	16.1	31.8	47.9
Earnings					
Lowest quartile	76.7	61.8	4.1	30.6	34.7
Second quartile	87.6	74.5	11.6	30.5	42.1
Third quartile	77.8	62.0	15.9	39.6	55.5
Fourth quartile	98.5	84.0	22.8	21.1	43.9
Occupation					
Managerial	87.1	80.2	4.3	22.4	26.7
Professional or technical	95.3	84.8	22.3	38.7	61.0
Sales, clerical, administrative support	89.3	72.5	10.2	23.2	33.4
Service	70.7	49.8	5.6	22.1	27.7
Production, operation	80.0	66.3	15.2	38.5	53.7
Tenure with employer					
Less than two years	73.3	67.5	8.9	56.5	65.4
Two to five years	74.8	56.8	4.5	19.5	24.0
Five to ten years	96.0	79.7	19.5	27.0	46.5
More than ten years	94.0	75.3	21.1	20.5	41.6

Source: 1995 survey of employer-provided training—employee results (1996a).
[a] Low turnover is less than 1 percent, medium turnover is 1 to 25 percent, and high turnover is more than 25 percent of average employment over previous three months.

In sum, the growing importance of workplace skills is reflected not only in growing returns to schooling in the workplace but also in an increase in formal employer-provided training over the past fifteen years. The United States nonetheless does less formal training in the workplace than do European and Japanese economies, which may be aggravated by rising displacement rates and other features of the U.S. employment system.

Employee Attitudes

How do employees perceive their job and their employer? Have these perceptions changed in recent years? One might expect that increased displacement risks would show up in increased worker anxiety and possibly decreased job satisfaction and employer commitment and loyalty. Such changes in attitudes could hurt economic performance, given the positive link between employee commitment and job performance (Kalleberg and Marsden 1995).

Although employee surveys at companies are common, nationally representative survey data on overall workforce trends are limited. Results from the general social survey (GSS), with data from 1973 to 1996, and several other sources show a general increase in perceived job insecurity, although no change in the perceived difficulty of finding another job. As mentioned, the percentage of workers believing that job loss in the next year is not at all likely was the same in the strong job growth year of 1996 as in the recession year of 1982, suggesting a general increase in job insecurity.[21] Employees in 1996 were, however, no more likely than in prior nonrecession years to say that it would be difficult to find another job with similar income and fringe benefits. Therefore, although many workers in the mid-1990s were still fearful of displacement, strong job growth had increased workers' confidence in finding a comparable job.[22]

Employee work satisfaction may have declined due to increased anxiety over displacement. Figure 2.6 shows a slight decline starting in the mid-1980s in the percentage of workers saying they are "very satisfied" with their work.[23] This is accounted for not by an increase in expressed dissatisfaction (which has changed little since the series began in 1972), but by an increase in workers saying they are only "moderately satisfied" with their work.[24]

- Some other surveys point toward a worsening of attitudes toward employers since the early 1980s (summarized in Cappelli et al. 1997, 199). Even among employees surviving downsizing and restructuring, studies find a drop in morale (Cascio 1993; Cappelli et al. 1997, 201). Almost two-thirds of Americans say that workers generally are less loyal to employers now than they were ten years ago, while only one-tenth say they are more loyal; correspondingly, three-fourths

Figure 2.6 Trends in Work Satisfaction, 1972 to 1996

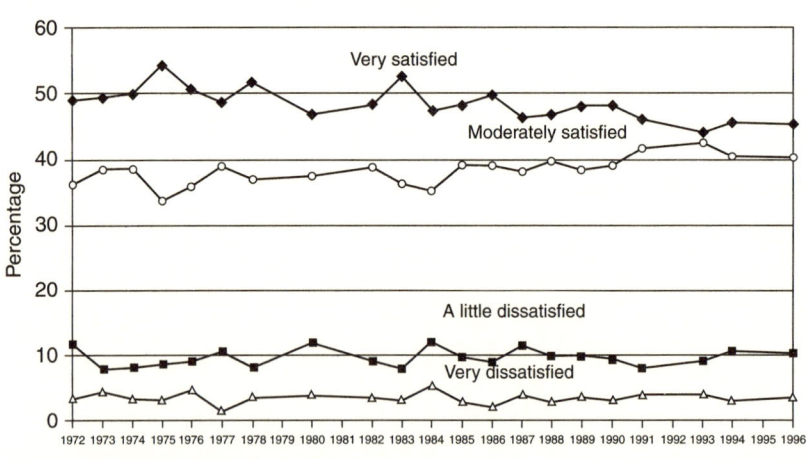

Source: general social survey.
Note: Percentages represent the distribution of employee answers to question, "On the whole, how satisfied are you with the work you do?"

say that employers are less loyal to employees than they were ten years ago.[25]

- Commitment to work in general, however, has stayed high, and a large number of U.S. employees express strong attachment to their employer. More than two-thirds of workers say they would continue working even if they did not need to, which has changed little in the past twenty-five years.[26] Also, employees are not more fatalistic: about two-thirds say that one's own hard work is more important than luck or help from others in getting ahead, which has risen slightly during this time period.[27] There also is no evidence of a decline in loyalty to one's immediate supervisor or in the percentage saying they trust their company to keep its promises.[28] About one-third of workers express strongly positive views of their employer, and only 10 percent express very negative views.[29]

What types of changes would employees like to see in the workplace? Recent polls show that one of the top employee concerns is pay (which is not surprising given the low growth in average wages over the past two decades). About three-fourths of employees feel that they should be paid more for their job, with one-sixth feeling that they should be paid over 20 percent more.[30] Three-fifths of Americans say that corporate mergers and downsizing have done more to keep wages down than to increase them—more than the number who say this about the North American Free Trade Agreement, the shift to a world economy, and the replacement of manufacturing by service jobs.[31]

Two-thirds of Americans feel that more job training services are needed and that the government should be doing more to help workers get job training and education.[32] A majority of workers would prefer to participate more in decisions as part of their job but feel that this responsibility cannot be acquired without some management initiative; about half of workers say that more rewarding tasks or responsibilities would make a difference in their job satisfaction.[33]

- Substantial segments of employees (between 20 and 50 percent in various polls) perceive the following problems: unfair roadblocks for many Americans even if they work hard; discrimination against women; greater divisions in society due to unequal access to education, training, and high-paying jobs; desire for a more understanding boss; difficulties in balancing work and family; too much pressure at work; low chances for promotion; lack of health insurance and other benefits; having to work long hours; and dissatisfaction with recognition for work accomplishments.[34]
- Many employees would like to participate more in company ownership. When asked to choose between a pay increase and a share in the ownership of the company, workers are split or tend to prefer an ownership share.[35] Given a 10 percent pay increase that could be taken in cash or company stock or a combination, only one-third of employees say that they would take it all in cash. A majority of Americans say that if they owned company stock, they would not vote to sell the company to an outside investor even for twice the market value of the stock.[36] In addition, employee ownership is seen to enhance company interests: four-fifths agree that employee stockholders are more likely than outside stockholders to vote their shares in the best long-term interests of the company. Participation in company decisions is, however, a crucial part of the support for employee ownership: three-fifths of Americans say that if they owned company stock, they would not be willing to let management vote their shares; also, given the choice between company stock and more input into company decisions, two-thirds say they would prefer more input into decisions.[37]

In sum, the evidence on attitudes indicates that there has been some general decline in job satisfaction and company loyalty over the past two decades, very likely connected to an increase in the perceived risk of job loss. Only a small minority, however, express dissatisfaction and low levels of attachment to employers. The most common employee concern is pay, but a majority of employees also express support for more training, more input into decisions, and more participation in company ownership. Such attitudes provide a good context for the next two sections, which explore these and other high-performance work practices.

Prevalence and Effects of High-Performance Work Practices

How work is organized can strongly affect workplace performance and the quality of the employee-employer relationship. While work organization may be built on and constrained by technological and market requirements, employers often have substantial latitude in choosing not only how to organize the work process but also what types of compensation and human resource policies to implement. The choices that employers make can reflect fundamental views of the role of employees in the workplace—whether employees are seen, at one extreme, as easily disposable factors of production whose motivation and commitment do not matter or, alternatively, as resources whose value to an organization can be enhanced through training, employee involvement, and other policies to enhance skills, motivation, and commitment. This section reviews the major research findings in this area along with available data on prevalence and recent trends in the use of various workplace policies and practices, including new evidence from an analysis of the 1994 and 1997 national employer surveys.

Prior Evidence

In the past decade new attention has been devoted to the role of workplace organization and human resource practices in outcomes for companies and employees. Employees often have knowledge and skills not available to managers and discretion over the level of their effort and the application of their knowledge and skills. The theoretical arguments and empirical research in this area focus on how certain practices or combinations of practices can enhance outcomes by building and drawing on employee skills, motivation, and commitment. Practices that may do so generally fall into five broad categories:

1. *Employee involvement*   Programs that solicit employee ideas and build involvement in the work process, such as self-managed teams and regular meetings to discuss work-related issues.
2. *Skill-building*   Formal and informal training and job rotation to build a broad range of skills.

3. *Reward systems* High compensation levels and individual and group-based incentives to reward workers for increased effort, cooperation, and sharing of skills and knowledge.
4. *Employment security* Explicit or implicit commitments by employers to provide long-term employment relationships.
5. *Rigorous recruitment and selection systems* Procedures that carefully assess the skills and personal qualities of applicants.

Several authors have argued that any one or two practices in these categories may have little, or even a negative, effect in the absence of the others (see Levine and Tyson 1990; Levine 1995; Huselid 1995). For example, employee involvement will not encourage workers to share ideas if they do not perceive that rewards of higher productivity will be shared (for example, through individual bonuses or group gain sharing) or if productivity gains are followed by worker layoffs (Levine and Tyson 1990). The success of employee involvement may also depend on a recruitment and selection system that produces employees who have or can develop good team skills. More generally, alignment of practices can send a consistent message to employees regarding valued behaviors in the organization (Jackson and Schuler 1995).

A number of empirical studies, using a variety of methodologies, provide support for the idea that human resource practices can substantially improve workplace performance and employee attitudes.[38] Based on the accumulated evidence, Casey Ichniowski and colleagues (1996, 322) conclude, "Innovative human resource practices can improve business productivity, primarily through the use of systems of related work practices designed to enhance worker participation and flexibility in the design of work and decentralization of managerial tasks and responsibilities." They also conclude that "new systems of participatory work practices have large, economically important effects" on business performance, while isolated changes in individual work practices do not generally improve performance.[39]

How many firms actually use the different policies and practices at the center of this discussion, and how many combine them in ways that these studies suggest are required to enhance motivation, commitment, and performance? Has this been changing in recent years? There is no long-running consistent data series that provides complete answers to these questions, although several sources provide valuable insights into recent use of such policies and practices. Here we briefly review evidence from several data sets based on broadly representative samples and then turn to recent national employer survey data that have richer detail.

Surveys of Fortune 1,000 companies indicate, as shown in table 2.7, some growth between 1987 and 1993 in the use of quality circles

Table 2.7 Innovative Workplace Policies and Practices in Use by U.S. Companies, 1987 to 1997 (Percentage of Companies)

Policy or Practice	Fortune 1,000 Companies			Public Companies	Medium and Large Establishments	Establishments (More Than Half of Workers Covered)	
	1987	1990	1993	1991	1993	1992	1997
Quality circles	61	66	65	61	5	27	58
Other participation groups	70	86	91				
Job enrichment or redesign	60	75	82	35			
Self-managed work teams	28	47	68	24	14	41	38
Job rotation					13	27	56
Total quality management	73	76			21	25	57
Survey response rate	51	32	28	60	71	65	58

Source: For Fortune 1,000 companies, Lawler, Mohrman, and Ledford 1995; for public companies surveyed in 1991, Kruse 1993; for establishments surveyed in 1993, Gittleman, Horrigan, and Joyce 1998; for establishments surveyed in 1992 and 1997, Osterman 1994, 2000. Medium and large establishments refer to those with more than fifty employees.

Note: Data cells are blank when the survey did not ask about that specific policy.

(problem-solving work teams focused on improving quality), other participation groups, job enrichment or redesign, and self-managed work teams (Lawler, Mohrman, and Ledford 1995). Most companies using these programs, though, cover only a minority of employees.[40] The numbers were slightly lower in a 1991 telephone survey of public companies that had a higher response rate than the Fortune 1,000 surveys (Kruse 1993).

Establishment-level surveys in 1992 and 1993 found a low incidence of four innovative work practices, although there was a doubling by 1997 in the prevalence of quality circles, job rotation, and total quality management covering more than half of core employees (Cappelli et al. 1997, 94; Gittleman, Horrigan, and Joyce 1998; Osterman 1994, 2000).[41] The practices were more common among firms emphasizing quality in their product market strategies (suggesting the importance of employee input for ensuring high quality), competing in international markets (suggesting increased exposure to these policies among international competitors), and introducing new technologies (Osterman 1994; Gittleman, Horrigan, and Joyce 1998). In 1997, five-sixths of firms had covered at least half of core employees by one or more of these practices, while one-sixth had covered them by all four. Firms with these practices were also more likely to have training and incentive compensation like profit sharing and bonuses, suggesting potential complementarities (Cappelli et al. 1997, 103; Gittleman, Horrigan, and Joyce 1998).

Based on the available evidence, the conclusions of Ichniowski et al. (1996) echo the earlier findings of the Commission on the Skills of the American Workforce (1990): a majority of U.S. businesses have adopted some forms of innovative work practices such as work teams and contingent compensation, but only a small percentage have combined these into a full system of innovative work practices (Ichniowski et al. 1996, 325).

New Evidence from National Employer Surveys

The data source that appears most representative of U.S. employers comes from the recent national employer surveys (NES). The NES was administered by the U.S. Census Bureau in 1994 and 1997 to human resource managers or plant managers in private sector for-profit establishments with twenty or more employees.[42] Tables 2.8 to 2.10 present a variety of numbers derived from these surveys. Although differences between the figures for 1994 and 1997 provide insights into recent workplace trends, only those differences with an asterisk between the figures should be taken as likely trends; the others are not strong enough to rule out sampling variability as an explanation for any difference between the figures.

70   A Working Nation

Table 2.8 reports a number of establishment characteristics in 1994 and 1997, broken down between manufacturing and nonmanufacturing firms and by unionization and employment size. Several findings are consistent with other studies:

- Computers are becoming more important in the workplace, with a rise in computer use among production workers as well as among managers and supervisors. Computer use in 1997 was especially high among managers or supervisors in the largest establishments and among production workers in nonmanufacturing establishments.
- More companies are using temporary and part-time workers. The percentage of establishments using temporary agency workers more than doubled (from 15 to 39 percent) from 1994 to 1997, with the highest use in manufacturing and large firms, while the percentage of firms using part-time workers increased more modestly (from 65 to 71 percent).
- Data on turnover illustrate some of the labor market pressures facing employers. About 20 percent of employees, on average, quit or retired within the previous year, and almost half of firms lost 10 percent or more of their employees to quits or retirements. Many fewer employees (averaging 6 percent) were lost to layoffs or firings.
- Pay levels increased between 1994 and 1997 by 7 to 11 percent across the employee categories, but employer provision of several types of benefits did not change significantly.[43]

Table 2.9 presents findings on work organization:

- About one-third of establishments have self-managed teams, half have job rotation, and three-fourths have work-related meetings for staff other than managers, all of which have become more popular in the past twenty years. Each of these programs is more common in manufacturing and large establishments. Almost all of the work-related meetings include the topics of working conditions, health and safety, and task improvement (even in nonunion establishments, where discussing working conditions with an employee organization is a violation of labor law), while only three-fifths report that these meetings cover the choice of new technology or equipment.
- Almost three-fourths of employers provided formal training to employees in the past year (consistent with the survey of employer-provided training data presented earlier), with the highest percentage among technical staff and the lowest among office, sales, and customer service staff. The percentage offering training in teamwork or problem-solving skills increased during this time,

perhaps reflecting more focus on workplace cooperation and employee discretion.
- Spending on recruitment and selection averaged 2.7 percent of labor costs in 1997, down from 4.6 percent in 1994 (despite the fact that the share of new employees was similar between the years, as shown in table 2.8).
- One-fifth of firms do benchmarking of practices and performance against other organizations.
- The number of organizational levels separating top officials and front-line supervisors, which many managers have tried to reduce in order to "flatten" organizational hierarchies, averaged slightly more than two in both 1994 and 1997.
- Close to one-fourth of establishments in 1997 reported reengineering within the previous three years, while more than one-third reported total quality management programs, flextime, and job sharing in 1994.

To what extent are these practices combined within workplaces? As noted, some theorists and researchers have emphasized the importance of combining policies, due to complementarities among them and the value of sending consistent signals regarding the role and value of employees. Although researchers have constructed several indexes of human resource practices, there is no standard index to be applied. Here we develop and present results from an eleven-point high-performance work practices index that includes many of the measures from tables 2.8 and 2.9. As described at the bottom of table 2.10, the index awards points both for new practices that have been promoted recently to increase performance and for traditional practices that reflect a strong investment in employees and attention to work practices.[44]

Table 2.10 presents findings on the combination of work practices:

- Despite frequent media attention and discussion, few firms combine many of the work practices. Almost half of establishments in both 1994 and 1997 have low scores (from zero to three) on the eleven-point index, while less than one-tenth have high scores of seven or more. The prevalence of high scores is slightly higher among manufacturing, unionized, and large establishments.
- High scores are more likely on the traditional practices index, although the percentage having high scores declined from 1994 to 1997. High scores are particularly likely among unionized establishments, where union members' higher pay levels and greater likelihood of pensions and health insurance exert a strong influence on the index.

Table 2.8 Workplace Characteristics, 1994 and 1997 (Percentage of Firms with Given Characteristic, Unless Otherwise Noted)

Characteristic	Overall 1994		Overall 1997
Computer use (average)			
Managers, supervisors	70.0	*	76.5
Production workers	41.9	*	52.1
Contingent workers			
Any temporary agency workers	14.8	*	39.4
Any part-time workers	64.8		70.6
Turnover in past year (average)			
Quit or retired	n.a.		19.9
Had more than 10 percent quit or retired	n.a.		46.2
Laid off or fired	n.a.		6.4
Had more than 10 percent laid off or fired	n.a.		16.8
Permanent employees with less than one year tenure (average)	20.5		21.6
Employment change in past three years			
Decreased	21.4	*	14.2
No change	40.5		48.4
Increased	38.1		39.4
Pay (average yearly, U.S. dollars)			
Managers or professionals[a]	41,509		46,848
Supervisors	30,817	*	34,067
Technicians	29,065		31,569
Office, sales, customer service	20,419		22,301
Production	21,264	*	22,895
Benefits			
Pension	56.9		60.2
Health insurance	90.6		90.6
Child care benefits	10.1		10.8
Stock options or profit sharing	n.a.		41.2
Stock options or profit sharing or bonuses	74.9		n.a.
Unionized	13.0	*	9.5
Manufacturing company	19.1		17.8
Establishment size			
20 to 49 employees	60.9		60.4
50 to 249 employees	33.9		34.6
250+ employees	5.2		5.0

Source: Based on establishment-level data from national employer surveys, waves I and II. Figures are weighted to reflect population.
* Difference between columns is statistically significant at $p < 0.05$.
[a] 1994 pay figure is just for managers.

The New Employee-Employer Relationship   73

	Industry, Unionization, and Size Breakdowns in 1997									
			Unionized			Number of Employees				
Manufacture		Nonmanufacture	Yes		No	20 to 49		50 to 249		250+
75.6		76.8	74.9		76.3	72.8	*	81.7	*	87.6
27.7	*	57.8	44.9		52.0	50.5		54.6		55.0
55.7	*	35.8	43.5		39.0	33.7	*	45.1	*	71.1
n.a.		n.a.	n.a.		n.a.	n.a.		n.a.		n.a.
12.7	*	21.5	10.9	*	20.9	17.8	*	24.1	*	17.1
31.7	*	49.5	25.7	*	48.4	45.4		48.2		42.3
6.8		6.2	6.0		6.4	6.1		6.9		6.1
15.2		17.1	14.1		17.1	17.0		16.6		15.1
14.5	*	23.1	13.4	*	22.4	21.3		22.5	*	18.3
18.1		13.4	16.9		14.0	12.4		16.3	*	23.7
39.7	*	47.9	51.1		45.9	49.2		44.1	*	27.5
42.3		38.8	32.0		40.2	38.5		39.6	*	48.8
51,207	*	45,897	57,007	*	45,863	45,070		49,296		52,544
37,212	*	33,149	45,915	*	32,793	33,459		34,498	*	37,297
34,569	*	30,557	36,562	*	30,951	29,956		32,873		34,837
25,263	*	21,459	26,498	*	21,819	21,954		22,674		23,354
24,203		22,564	30,901	*	22,067	22,393		23,347	*	25,893
67.8	*	58.5	84.7	*	57.6	51.5	*	72.8	*	79.8
95.9	*	89.5	98.7	*	89.8	86.5	*	96.8		99.1
7.0	*	11.7	12.3		10.7	7.4	*	15.7		19.8
45.3		40.4	49.7		40.3	35.6		49.4		55.4
n.a.		n.a.	n.a.		n.a.	n.a.		n.a.		n.a.
17.6	*	7.8	100.0		0.0	5.9		13.8	*	24.4
100.0		0.0	32.9	*	16.2	13.9		21.6	*	38.6
47.2	*	63.3	37.9	*	63.4	100.0		0.0		0.0
41.9	*	33.0	49.5	*	32.5	0.0		100.0		0.0
10.9	*	3.8	12.6	*	4.1	0.0		0.0		100.0

Table 2.9 Workplace Organization, 1994 and 1997 (Percentage of Establishments with Given Policy or Feature, Unless Otherwise Noted)

Characteristic	Overall 1994		Overall 1997
Self-managed teams for nonmanagers			
Any	31.8		34.3
If any, percentage employees covered (average)	41.1		45.3
More than 50 percent of nonmanagers covered	8.6		12.3
Work-related meetings for nonmanagers			
Any	80.3		74.3
If any, percentage employees covered (average)	65.1	*	74.6
More than 50 percent of nonmanagers covered	47.9		52.5
If have meetings, topics include:			
Working conditions	90.3		90.6
Health and safety	89.5		92.7
Choice of new technology or equipment	59.2		59.6
Task improvement	97.8		97.8
Job rotation for nonmanagers			
Any	49.3		47.7
If any, percentage of employees covered (average)	40.2		45.5
More than 50 percent of nonmanagers covered	14.1		16.5
Formal training in past year for:			
Any employees	79.9		72.4
Managers or professionals[a]	69.6	*	60.3
Supervisors	n.a.		61.0
Technical staff	35.2	*	70.4
Office, sales, customer service staff	48.8		52.5
Production workers	61.4		60.6
Teamwork or problem-solving training	54.8	*	62.7
Recruitment as percent of total labor costs (average)	4.6	*	2.7
Benchmarking against other organizations	22.5		20.4
Levels between front-line supervisor and top official (average)	2.12		2.08
Reengineering in past three years	n.a.		24.5
Total quality management program	39.5		n.a.
Flextime for any employees	36.6		n.a.
Job sharing for any employees	35.3		n.a.

Source: Based on establishment-level data from national employer surveys, waves I and II. Figures are weighted to reflect population.
* Difference between columns is statistically significant at $p < .05$.
[a] 1994 training figure is for managers or supervisors.

Industry, Unionization, and Size Breakdowns in 1997

Manufacture		Nonmanufacture	Unionized			Number of Employees				
			Yes		No	20 to 49		50 to 249		250+
35.7		34.0	38.9		34.3	31.4		37.7	*	46.5
46.1		45.2	39.8		46.0	52.0		37.0		36.6
12.6		12.2	11.7		12.5	13.2		10.5		12.5
78.3		73.5	72.6		74.7	69.5	*	81.0	*	87.7
63.9	*	77.1	58.9	*	76.1	80.8	*	66.0		69.5
44.9	*	54.1	38.7		53.9	53.8		49.3	*	58.9
85.4	*	91.8	87.2		90.9	92.7	*	88.7	*	82.7
94.6		92.3	96.2	*	92.4	94.2		91.3		87.3
51.8	*	61.4	56.0		60.0	62.3		55.0	*	63.1
93.2	*	98.9	96.0		98.0	98.8		96.3		97.9
54.2	*	46.3	42.9		48.9	46.4		49.3		53.9
46.7		45.2	38.3		46.1	53.0		34.8		34.2
18.5		16.1	12.3		17.2	19.8	*	11.1		13.1
71.4		72.7	74.2		72.3	69.2		76.1	*	87.4
60.4		60.3	58.8		60.5	53.4	*	69.2	*	84.5
58.8		61.7	56.0		61.6	56.5		64.6	*	82.7
64.3		72.4	70.8		70.4	71.3		67.1	*	81.9
51.9		52.7	57.6		52.0	46.8	*	57.5	*	79.5
55.7		61.8	62.8		60.4	56.5		65.2	*	79.8
58.3		63.7	59.0		63.1	58.6		67.4	*	81.6
2.2		2.9	2.3		2.8	2.4		3.3		4.2
22.3		19.9	23.0		20.1	15.6	*	26.2	*	39.3
2.01		2.09	2.32		2.05	1.86	*	2.31	*	3.14
26.5		24.5	28.9		24.4	20.4	*	29.9	*	44.9
n.a.		n.a.	n.a.		n.a.	n.a.		n.a.		n.a.
n.a.		n.a.	n.a.		n.a.	n.a.		n.a.		n.a.
n.a.		n.a.	n.a.		n.a.	n.a.		n.a.		n.a.

Table 2.10 High-Performance Work Practices Index (Percentage of Firms)

			Industry, Unionization, and Size Breakdowns in 1997						
	Overall				Unionized		Number of Employees		
Index	1994	1997	Manufacture	Nonmanufacture	Yes	No	20 to 49	50 to 249	250+
Index (0 to 11)									
Low (0 to 3)	48.7	47.1	46.9	47.1	44.0	45.7	53.0 *	38.7	32.7
Medium (4 to 6)	43.1	44.7	45.7	44.5	47.1	45.9	41.0	49.4 *	56.9
High (7 to 11)	8.2	8.2	7.5	8.4	9.0	8.4	6.0 *	11.9	10.4
Traditional practices index (0 to 4)									
Low (0 to 1)	50.8 *	60.3	55.9	61.3	47.0 *	60.5	68.2 *	49.9	37.3
Medium (2)	33.2	28.4	31.3	27.8	35.0	28.6	23.7 *	34.9	41.2
High (3 to 4)	16.1 *	11.3	12.8	10.9	18.1 *	10.9	8.1	15.3 *	21.5
New practices index (0 to 7)									
Low (0 to 2)	59.2 *	51.1	57.1	49.8	57.4	49.0	53.3	47.7	48.9
Medium (3 to 4)	33.3	41.1	36.4	42.2	35.6	43.0	39.7	43.3	43.2
High (5 to 7)	7.5	7.8	6.5	8.0	7.0	8.1	7.0	9.1	7.9

Self-managed teams, work-related meetings,
and job rotation for nonmanagers

All three	16.7	19.1	22.0	*	18.4	17.9	19.8	17.2	21.0	*	27.9
Less than 50 percent in each	2.1	1.4	3.0	*	1.1	2.6	1.4	1.0	1.9		3.3

Source: Based on establishment-level data from national employer surveys, waves I and II. Figures are weighted to reflect population.
* Difference between columns is statistically significant at $p<.05$.
Note: Full index for high-performance work practices includes one point for each of the following eleven practices:
1. More than 50 percent of nonmanagers are in self-managed teams.
2. More than 50 percent of nonmanagers are in regular work-related meetings.
3. More than 50 percent of nonmanagers are in job rotation.
4. Formal training programs are available for each employee category.
5. Training covering teamwork or problem-solving skills.
6. Number of levels between front-line supervisor and top official is no higher than median level for size class.
7. Recruitment and selection expenditures are higher than average for companies with similar number of new workers.
8. Profit sharing or stock options are available to employees.
9. Mean compensation levels are higher than industry averages for each employee category.
10. Pensions and medical insurance are available to employees.
11. Benchmarking programs compare practices and performance with those of other organizations.

New practices index includes just the first seven of the above practices, while the traditional practices index includes just the practices eight through eleven. See text for further discussion.

- Less than one-tenth of establishments have high scores on the new practices index, which did not change significantly between 1994 and 1997. A number of firms with low scores in 1994, however, added practices so that there was significant growth in the medium-score category in 1997. Separating out three of the new practices—self-managed teams, work-related meetings, and job rotation for staff other than managers—the percentage having all three did not change significantly between the two years.

What do we make of the finding that few firms appear to extensively combine practices that are viewed as ingredients of high-performance workplaces (also concluded by Ichniowski et al. 1996) and that this number has not been increasing recently? Assuming that the measures used here are good ones and that the research finding positive outcomes is valid, two broad interpretations are possible.[45] The first is that information problems limit their diffusion: employers are not sufficiently aware of the benefits of these policies or of how to combine them in productive ways in the workplace. Given that the field of research is young, this lack of information is not surprising.

A second interpretation is that employers face significant barriers or other costs in adopting high-performance work practices. One barrier could be organizational inertia and sunk costs—once a work process and an organizational hierarchy are established, it can be difficult to change established tasks, positions, or relationships by implementing (for example) self-managed work teams or undertaking reengineering that reduces the layers of management. Another barrier may be lack of managerial time and other resources to implement changes, particularly in smaller firms. Changing workplace practices may be a risky investment with uncertain payoffs, which also could dissuade small firms operating at the margin. Apart from these barriers within the firm, a firm's environment also may impose barriers or higher costs (Levine and Tyson 1990; Levine 1992). As noted in the discussion of training, financial markets may undervalue investments in worker training and new work practices, due to measurement problems and the inability to use intangible worker skills or new working relationships as collateral. As another example, in a labor market with substantial job insecurity, firms offering more secure jobs may attract a disproportionate number of low-quality workers desiring protection against layoffs or firings; such firms will not capture the positive externalities for workers and society from lower levels of layoffs. Such factors can make a case for public policy to decrease the barriers or otherwise help firms overcome the barriers to adopting more secure, participative, and productive work arrangements (Levine 1992).

Employee Participation in Ownership and Profits

Over the past twenty years there has been growing interest in and use of employee ownership, profit-sharing, and gain-sharing plans in U.S. workplaces. Along with many of the practices discussed in the previous section, these have attracted interest for their potential to improve workplace performance by strengthening incentives for productive cooperation and information sharing. In addition, employee ownership has attracted interest for its potential to broaden the distribution of wealth, while profit sharing has attracted interest for its potential to decrease layoffs and stabilize employment. This section provides an overview of available evidence on the incidence and effects of employee ownership, profit sharing, and gain sharing.

Employee Ownership

There is general support for employee ownership, shown in part by the finding that workers are as likely to prefer a share of company ownership as a pay increase and by the finding that a majority of Americans say they would not sell stock in their employer even to an outside investor offering twice the market value. There are four major types of employee ownership:

- *Employee stock ownership plans (ESOPs)* These were first given recognition and special tax treatment as a form of pension plan in the 1974 Employee Retirement Income Security Act (ERISA). The principal legislative sponsor was Senator Russell Long, who saw them primarily as a way to broaden the overall distribution of wealth. The most recent data indicate that 6.5 million workers, representing 6.4 percent of the private sector workforce, are participating in more than 8,700 ESOPs with combined assets of $223 billion (Department of Labor 1998, 55). Almost one-fourth of ESOP participants are in collectively bargained ESOPs.

- *Other pensions holding employer stock* Just over 8 million workers are participating in non-ESOP defined-contribution pension plans that hold a total of $91 billion of employer stock.[46] 401(k) plans, which allow or require employee contributions, have become a major factor in employer stock: 6.9 million participants, or 30 percent of all participants, have employer stock held in large 401(k) plans. One-third of 401(k) participants holding employer stock do so in plans that combine a 401(k) with an ESOP (often called a KSOP), since the 401(k) option can be applied to ESOP as well as non-ESOP plans. Altogether, 401(k) plans account for 69 percent of all employer stock held in defined-contribution plans and more than 80 percent of employer stock held by non-ESOP plans.

- *Stock purchase or stock option programs* Employer stock was owned directly by 9 percent of employees in 1983 (Brickley and Hevert 1991). Broad-based stock options grew in popularity in the 1990s, with 2,000 to 3,000 public companies providing stock options to employees other than managers (National Center for Employee Ownership 1998).

- *Worker cooperatives* These are organized on a one person—one vote basis and tend to be limited to small companies (Jones 1979; Bonin, Jones, and Putterman 1993).

Combining the various methods of owning employer stock, about one-fifth of American adults report holding stock in the company in which they work.[47] Close to one-third of adult shareholders report owning their employer's stock, while a similar number report getting their start in stockholding through a company stock plan.[48]

Although a large number of U.S. employees own employer stock, almost all of this stock is in firms that are minority employee-owned. Of U.S. companies with more than ten employees, approximately 2,000 have a majority of stock owned by their employees.[49] Among large public companies, only a few are majority employee-owned (United Airlines most prominently), but among public companies generally (where the Securities and Exchange Commission defines a 5 percent stockholder as a major stakeholder) almost 1,000 have more than 4 percent of stock held broadly by employees, with average employee holdings of 12 percent (Blasi and Kruse 1991). There has been substantial growth of public firms with more than 20 percent of broad employee ownership (Blair et al. 2000).

What role does employee ownership play in the workplace? In the past twenty years there have been more than sixty large-sample research studies of the effects of employee ownership, including twenty-six studies of employee attitudes and behavior, twenty-nine studies of firm productivity and profitability, and seven studies of employment and sales growth and behavior. Many of the studies used not just cross-sectional comparisons, but comparisons before and after the adoption of employee ownership, allowing one to be more confident of causality.

Our review of the employee ownership studies (Kruse and Blasi 1997) finds the following:

- Employee attitudes and behavior may be either improved or unchanged under employee ownership. Organizational commitment and identification are higher under employee ownership in most studies, while findings are mixed between favorable and neutral on job satisfaction, motivation, and behavioral measures.[50] The findings of positive attitudes under employee ownership generally are not linked to the size of one's ownership stake, but they often are linked to employee participation in decisions, suggesting that such participation can increase a sense of ownership. Despite this, most results indicate that perceived or desired employee participation generally did not increase under employee ownership, and there is no evidence of decreases in the need or desire for union representation under employee ownership.[51]

- Firm performance studies also are split between neutral and favorable findings. Although the majority of studies cannot reject the null hypothesis of no significant relationship between employee ownership and performance, our meta-analysis of the ESOP studies finds that we can reject this null hypothesis overall based on the disproportionate number of positive and significant estimates. The average estimated productivity difference between ESOP and non-ESOP firms is 6 percent, and the average estimated productivity increase in the year of ESOP adoption is 4 percent; average productivity growth following adoption is similar between ESOP and non-ESOP firms. Analysis of worker cooperatives also has linked several cooperative features to better firm performance.

- Several studies find higher employment growth among employee ownership companies, particularly where there is a high level of employee participation in decisions.

- The stock prices of employee ownership companies tend to do better than those of other public companies. An index of public firms with more than 10 percent employee ownership has generally beat stock market indexes since it began in 1992 (American Capital Strategies 1998); firms with more than 5 percent employee ownership in 1991 had higher stock price growth than otherwise-similar firms over the 1980s (Blasi, Conte, and Kruse 1996); and a portfolio of public firms that were more than 20 percent employee-owned in 1983 performed better, with lower risk, than a matched portfolio of otherwise-similar firms without employee ownership (Blair, Kruse, and Blasi 2000). This indicates that employer stock is not a bad investment in general, although clearly employees need to minimize financial risk by having other investments.

These results led us to the following basic conclusions: employee ownership does not magically and automatically improve employee attitudes, behavior, and firm performance whenever it is implemented, and there are a number of findings that employee attitudes, behavior, and firm performance are either improved or unaffected by employee ownership, while it is rare to find worse attitudes or performance under employee ownership.

These conclusions fly in the face of both very rosy views and highly unfavorable views of employee ownership. Quite simply, employee ownership has become a part of many workplaces without making a difference in how employees are treated or how work is done. At a minimum, the results indicate that a substantial expansion of employee ownership will not hurt overall economic performance. Although the studies provide some hints of what can enhance the effects of employee ownership—in particular, employee participation in decisions may be important—too little is known about the salient organizational mechanisms that can explain the connections between employee ownership, attitudes, and performance.

Two recent studies provide important insights into employee outcomes under employee ownership. Comparisons of firms with and without employee ownership find that ESOPs appear to improve worker wealth, coming on top of (rather than at the expense of) regular pay and other benefits. They do not, however, appear to affect the distribution of pay within firms (Kardas, Scharf, and Keogh 1998). Employee ownership firms have higher survival rates and more stable employment than other firms, suggesting that large employee ownership stakes may lead to formal or informal pressure to minimize displacement and enhance long-term employment relationships (Blair et al. 2000). Both studies suggest important potential for employee ownership to improve the well-being of workers.[52]

Profit Sharing

Profit sharing has attracted interest in the United States for more than two hundred years, receiving support from Thomas Jefferson's treasury secretary, Albert Gallatin, and eminent nineteenth-century scholars such as John Stuart Mill and William Stanley Jevons. Gallatin saw it as a way to "extend the democratic principle upon which this Nation was founded . . . to the industrial operation," while many proponents in the nineteenth and early twentieth centuries saw it as a way to strengthen capitalism against the competing communist and socialist ideologies (U.S. Senate 1939; Kruse 1993, 1–2). The principal argument for profit sharing, however, has been that it can align the incentives of employees and owners by motivating employees to create higher profits through improved productivity (or as put in 1939 Senate hearings, "bringing into harmonious cooperation all the operating and productive factors of the company operation" (U.S. Senate 1939, 65). This theory received new attention in the past two decades due to concerns about lagging productivity growth.

A second argument, developed fully in the 1980s, is that profit sharing can aid economic stability and decrease unemployment. Martin Weitzman's share economy theory holds that by changing the incentives of firms to hire and retain workers, widespread profit sharing would lead to greater macroeconomic stability, fewer recessionary pressures, and lower unemployment levels (Weitzman 1984). Because the gains from employment stability accrue not just to the profit-sharing firm but also to the economy as a whole, this theory presents a case for public policy to encourage profit sharing.

About one-fifth of U.S. firms and employees participate in some type of profit sharing.[53] The prevalence is higher among publicly held firms where profits are public information: close to two-fifths of public firms have profit sharing for employees (Kruse 1993, 8–10). Most profit sharing is deferred, where the profit share is put into an employee retirement account, while about one-fifth of participants are in cash-only plans, and another one-tenth are in cash or deferred plans where the employees can elect to defer their profit share. Profit-sharing formulas vary widely among companies—a variety of profit measures and thresholds are used to determine the profit share, with many companies making the share discretionary from year to year.

What are the effects of profit sharing on firms and employees? The principal findings of prior studies are the following:

- Employees tend to be favorably disposed toward profit sharing, with positive views of its effects on employee loyalty, work effort, and other measures (Weitzman and Kruse 1990, 115–18). Absenteeism and quits are lower in profit-sharing firms (Wilson and Peel 1991), suggesting higher worker commitment.[54] However, many employees also express reservations about income variability, agreeing that profit sharing "can cause bitterness or disappointment, because profits can go down as well as up."

- Profit sharing is consistently linked to better firm performance. Across thirty studies with 345 estimates, 92 percent of the estimates indicate a positive relationship between profit sharing and productivity or profitability, and meta-analysis clearly rejects the null hypothesis of no relationship (Bell and Kruse 1995).[55] The findings are strongest for before and after post studies where, as with ESOPs, productivity goes up an average of 4 to 5 percent in the year of adoption, while productivity growth following adoption is similar to that of other firms (Kruse 1993).

- Studies are mixed on the stabilizing potential of profit sharing. About half of the findings from the nineteen studies on this topic are generally favorable regarding the stabilizing effects of profit sharing, while the remainder are split between mixed and unfavorable findings (Kruse 1998, 109–13).[56] Therefore, a number of studies indicate that profit sharing may have important employment-stabilizing effects, but there is no strong consensus as there is in the literature on firm performance.

Gain Sharing

A gain-sharing plan ties a portion of employee compensation to a group operational measure—such as output, productivity, quality, safety, or costs—rather than to a financial measure such as profitability or returns. These plans often involve employees in some formal way to develop ideas and skills for improving performance. The three most popular types are Scanlon, Rucker, and ImproShare plans, although the number of custom-designed plans is growing.[57] Data on their use are sparse. The Fortune 1,000 surveys found 26 percent of companies in 1987 and 42 percent in 1993 with gain-sharing plans somewhere in the company, although most included less than 20 percent of employees (Lawler, Mohrman, and Ledford 1995, 19). Broader surveys of compensation and human resource managers found 14 percent of companies in 1986 and 13 percent of companies in 1991 reporting gain-sharing plans.[58] Although there are no aggregate estimates, the percentage of employees covered is likely to be low since most firms with gain sharing include only a minority of employees.

What are the effects of gain-sharing plans? Although there have been a number of case studies of gain-sharing programs, there has been no analysis of large data sets comparing companies with and without such plans. Most of the case studies have shown positive effects on group performance (summarized in Collins 1998, 16–17), and a meta-analysis of thirty-three case studies finds improved outcomes for employees and firms in 67 to 91 percent of the cases (Bullock and Tubbs 1990).[59] Several studies using pre and post comparisons and objective productivity measures find higher productivity after gain sharing is adopted (Schuster 1983, 1984; Kaufman 1992; Hansen 1997); in particular, Kaufman (1992) finds a sustained median increase of more than 17 percent three years following the adoption of ImproShare. As with profit sharing, employees and employers involved in gain-sharing plans tend to have strongly positive attitudes about gain sharing.

In contrast to studies of profit sharing and employee ownership, substantial attention has been paid to how gain-sharing plans work. The studies tend to find that greater success is associated with high employee involvement in design and operation, shorter payout periods, productivity-based rewards, controllable targets, use of outside consultants, favorable employee views and managerial commitment when the program is implemented, and perceptions of procedural and distributive justice (Bullock and Tubbs 1990; Welbourne, Balkin, and Gómez-Mejía 1995; Kim 1996; Collins 1998). There is, however, no simple formula predicting success: Collins concludes from six generally successful case studies that outcomes often depend on internal organizational politics (Collins 1998, 201–32).

Diffusion of Plans

The research on employee ownership, profit sharing, and gain sharing strongly points toward better average performance for firms adopting these plans. The average productivity increase of 4 to 5 percent in the year following the adoption of an ESOP or profit-sharing plan may seem small, but it is more than three times the average annual productivity growth in the United States in the past twenty-five years. Many of the studies of employee outcomes point toward greater job satisfaction, higher pay, and lower likelihood of layoff. Although it is clear that adoption of these plans does not automatically result in better outcomes for workers or firms, the paucity of unfavorable research findings is noteworthy, indicating little risk that these systems will lead to worse outcomes.

Given these findings, why have not more firms adopted ESOPs, profit-sharing, and gain-sharing plans? Research on ESOPs and profit sharing has revealed a wide variety of reasons for their adoption; most firms say that they do so to improve productivity or employee benefits, while many firms point toward reducing turnover or (for ESOPs) tax advantages, buying out existing owners, and raising capital for investment (with very few citing wage concessions or saving failing firms; General Accounting Office 1986; Kruse 1993). Although some studies have found a few objective predictors of adoption, the weak role played by predictors along with disparate findings across studies indicate that a large role is played by managerial discretion and circumstances of the individual company (Kruse 1996).

As with the discussion of high-performance work practices, there are two interpretations of the fact that only a minority of workers are covered by these plans (assuming that the strong consensus of research findings is correct). One is that information problems limit their diffusion. In particular, although outcomes under these plans may be good on average, many plans do not produce better outcomes, and the research so far has not strongly identified how specific factors in structuring and implementing plans affect success (particularly for ESOPs and profit-sharing plans).

A second interpretation is that there are important barriers or other costs in adopting employee ownership, profit-sharing, and gain-sharing plans. Such barriers might include organizational inertia or lack of managerial time and resources to gather information and implement new systems. Specific barriers to the implementation of employee ownership and profit sharing may include worker concerns about variable income (which must be balanced against the possible reduction in the risks of layoff) and managerial concerns about employee expectations for information and participation in decisions (particularly if implemented in the absence of information-sharing and participative mechanisms). Also, teamwork training is probably very important for enhancing performance under collective reward systems, and financial markets may undervalue investments in training or other changes in human resources needed to optimize performance. The public policy implications of this evidence and these interpretations are discussed in the final section.

Summary and Public Policy for the New Employee-Employer Relationship

Have we seen a weakening of the employee-employer relationship in the United States in recent years? This chapter reviewed a wide range of evidence on whether and how the employment relationship has been changing, and on workplace policies and practices that may enhance both employer and employee interests. Some of the principal finding are:

- The risk of displacement has grown for workers in the 1990s, particularly for white-collar and service workers, and the costs of displacement for the average worker remain substantial. Corporate reorganizations and automation account for an increased share of extended layoffs, while the shares due to import competition and business relocation have not increased.
- While temporary help agency employment has grown in the past decade, the overall number of contingent workers desiring noncontingent arrangements has not increased. Somewhere between 2 percent and 8 percent of workers are in contingent jobs with substantial risk of job loss, which has decreased in the tight labor market of the late 1990s
- Between two-thirds and three-fourths of employees and employers are involved in formal training programs, but U.S. employees receive less job training that do their European and Japanese counterparts.

- Job satisfaction, employer commitment, and loyalty measures have declined somewhat since the mid-1980s, although commitment to work remains high and most workers still express attachment to their employers. Majorities of workers express desires for more pay, training, and input into workplace decisions.

A number of firms in the past two decades have implemented workplace practices designed to increase employee involvement in and commitment to their jobs and companies, more fully developing and drawing on employee knowledge and skills. The review of existing evidence plus new evidence from the Census Bureau surveys found that while many firms adopt individual practices, only a small minority actually combine these practices to create higher-performance workplaces that can significantly enhance business performance.

Employee participation in ownership and profits has often been promoted not only to enhance workplace cooperation and business performance, but also to increase employment stability and broaden the distribution of wealth. Our review of evidence in this area finds that about one-fifth of U.S. workers own their employer's stock, one-fifth are involved in profit sharing, while a smaller number are involved in group performance-based gain-sharing plans. While these plans do not automatically improve firm performance and employee attitudes, performance and attitudes strongly tend to be better on average. Productivity goes up in the year an ESOP or profit-sharing plan is adopted by an average of 4 to 5 percent (three times the annual average productivity growth in the United States over the past twenty-five years), and higher productivity is sustained in following years with productivity growth rates similar to that of other firms. In addition, many studies find lower layoffs and increased stability under profit sharing, while some evidence indicates that employee ownership may also enhance stability and survival of firms.

The evidence assembled here does not support the popular idea that there has been a fairly rapid, wholesale shift in employment relationships in the 1990s. It does, however, point to some trends that are cause for concern about the direction of employee-employer relationships.

It is possible to envision two fundamentally different paths that the employee-employer relationship can take in the United States in the next twenty years.[60] One path continues the trend of job insecurity as firms respond to high levels of competition and technological change by weakening connections to any one group of employees—by treating workers as a variable cost who can be readily laid off or hired on a contingent basis in response to often-rapid changes in markets and technologies. In this arrangement, firms focus on the current skills that employees can provide and are unlikely to invest in employee training or in policies and benefits that encourage worker commitment. A second path has firms strengthening employee-employer connections in order to develop a highly skilled and committed workforce that is an important resource in adapting to changes in markets and technologies. In this arrangement firms use extensive training, employee involvement, and flexible reward systems to create and take advantage of workers' higher-level skills, motivation, and commitment.

The next twenty years will undoubtedly contain plenty of examples of firms taking both paths. We base our discussion of public policy on what can be done to enhance the second path—to create high-performance workplaces where workers and employers share the rewards of high performance, workers have employment security and high levels of skill, and firms have productive, committed workforces. The policy recommendations we offer are meant to be provocative, to stimulate discussion of what the employee-employer relationship should look like and how that can be achieved.

As shown in this chapter, existing research provides substantial support for positive performance effects from employee participation in ownership, profits, and other high-performance work practices. Why then are they not used more frequently, particularly in combination with one another? As discussed, informational and other barriers may limit the diffusion of these practices; such barriers may be addressed by public policies aimed at encouraging these systems. The agricultural extension system, for example, is justified by the public good of spreading information to farmers, ensuring that productive innovations are diffused quickly. Government-sponsored demonstration projects may be similarly justified both in testing and diffusing knowledge of innovations. In addition, existing laws and regulations can be reviewed with an eye toward removing obstacles to innovative practices; for example, uncertainty over the legality of some forms of employee participation in nonunion settings has made a majority of managers cautious about expanding such programs (Commission on the Future of Worker Management Relations 1994, 53).

A different type of public policy rationale is provided when certain behaviors or practices have positive externalities or societal benefits not captured by the actors. Although the benefits of productivity improvements are captured within the firm, there may be important societal benefits in the spread of profit sharing and employee ownership. This is particularly true for the share economy theory of profit sharing: gains from employment stability accrue to the entire economy, as macroeconomic stability is enhanced by the maintenance of worker output and purchasing power without unemployment benefits or government assistance.

This can provide a strong case for tax incentives to encourage firms and workers to use profit sharing (Weitzman 1984; Mitchell 1995). A different type of rationale has been used to support public policy favoring employee ownership, in which it is seen as a "merit good" or as serving a "social transformation" role (Mitchell 1995). Senator Russell Long was an early proponent of ESOPs on the basis that they could help to broaden the distribution of wealth in the United States. Viewed as an intrinsic good or as having important social consequences (such as keeping society from splitting further into the haves and have-nots), a more equal distribution of wealth through employee ownership may justify favorable public policy (as argued, for example, by Gates 1998).

Our policy ideas are based on several findings about the direction of employee-employer relations. Career-long commitment of companies to employees appears to be on the decline; nevertheless, companies often voice demands for more performance, more skill, more commitment, and more flexibility from the workers who remain on the job. Also, most employees voice a desire for greater participation on their jobs, and there is widespread support for employee ownership and performance-based pay. In other words, the notion of an ongoing economic partnership between American workers and American companies—a kind of employee-led capitalism—has strong support. Despite all this, only a small minority of U.S. firms involve employees extensively in ownership, profits, and a combination of high-performance work practices. Research findings indicate that significant expansion of these practices could boost overall economic performance; at a minimum, there is no support for the view that their widespread use would harm performance.

Given these findings and the positive role that public policy may play both in overcoming informational and other barriers and in encouraging practices with societal benefits, we offer the following specific policy ideas to stimulate discussion and debate. In fashioning these, we have tried to adhere to the principle that policy recommendations must be simple and easy to understand for companies, employees, government officials, and the general public if they are to have any chance of adoption.

Better documentation of high-performance work practices is needed, given their potential for increasing U.S. business performance. There is no current method for annual documentation of high-performance work practices, and they cannot be encouraged and studied well if they cannot be measured and tracked. Therefore we offer two recommendations:

1. Establish a national commission of business, labor, and government representatives to mobilize expertise, serve as an information clearinghouse, and sponsor objective research on work practices (similar to the government's role in health and safety research).

2. Collect more data through the Bureau of Labor Statistics or the Census Bureau, and possibly through business tax returns, to gather better information on high-performance work practices: (1) How much of the company's common and preferred stock was owned by different classes of employees, and what was the value of stock and stock options distributed to different classes of employees last year? Under what format was stock distributed (ESOP, 401[k], and stock purchase), and what percentage of employees participated? (2) How much of the company's W-2 compensation was distributed through profit-sharing or gain-sharing plans to different classes of employees in the past year, and what percentage of employees of each class participated in this program? What was the specific format of this profit sharing or gain sharing? (3) How many employees in different categories participated in formal employee involvement structures, such as self-managed work teams, and did employees below top management have bona fide representatives on the board of directors? (4) How much was spent on worker training and on recruitment and selection, both overall and for specific classes of employees? (5) What types of pension and health insurance packages were offered to employees?

Tax incentives for profit sharing may be justified to encourage employment-stabilizing systems, while ESOP incentives are based on the value of broadening the distribution of wealth and encouraging greater employee participation in the economic system. In addition, some targeted incentives may be justified to help firms overcome informational and other barriers to the adoption of new work practices. We offer the following ideas for consideration:

3. Enhance, expand, and increase the basic tax benefit for all employee ownership plans, broadened stock option plans, and profit-sharing and gain-sharing plans to offer firms a meaningful incentive to increase the involvement of employees in the business.

4. Drive a meaningful proportion of any further decreases in the business tax (either reduced tax rates or increased tax credit) mainly by tax reductions based on the adoption of multiple high-performance work practices. These can be based on the combination of the following grades of high-performance workplace practices: (1) more than 30 percent (or alternatively, 15 percent) of W-2 compensation for all classes of employees spent on employee-owned stock, stock options, profit sharing, or gain sharing, (2) more than 50 percent of employees in self-managed work teams, (3) a high percentage of annual labor costs spent on training, (4) high expenditures on recruitment and selection costs for a given number of job openings, (5) at

least one rank-and-file or supervisory employee or a representative on the board of directors, (6) a minimum health insurance and pension package, and (7) an alternative dispute resolution program that ends in binding arbitration for all employees.

Most basically, such policies would allow the public to track the development of the new employment relationship and provide incentives for valuable innovations. We see these ambitious recommendations as initiatives that can help to reshape the nature of the typical employee-employer relationship for the twenty-first century, creating high-performance shared capitalism and avoiding a system based on job insecurity, inadequate worker skills, and low levels and growth of productivity.

Chapter 3

Creating Good Jobs and Good Wages

ALL IN ALL, this seems like a strange time to be concerned about good jobs and good wages in the American economy. Total civilian employment has increased about 175,000 a month for more than seven years, and the employment rate is at a record high. As of October 1999 the unemployment rate was 4.1 percent, the lowest since the late 1960s, and the median period of unemployment was only 6.4 weeks. The number of major strikes has declined to an annual rate about one-tenth that of the 1960s. Although the growth of productivity and average real compensation was sluggish for many years, both have increased at a 2+ percent annual rate since 1995. Moreover, the inflation rate is at its lowest level since the early 1960s, increasing the prospect that these conditions may continue indefinitely. Current macroeconomic conditions in the United States are the envy of the world.

Now is an appropriate time, however, to focus on the longer-term trends and perceived problems in the U.S. labor market. Two conditions merit special attention:

1. The annual increases in (measured) productivity and average real compensation were unusually low in the period from 1974 through 1995.
2. The variance of wages by skill level increased substantially during this same period.

These two trends and the government policies that might affect them are the focus of this chapter.

Major Developments Affecting Employment and Earnings

Changes in consumer demand and relative productivity have led to substantial changes in the composition of employment. Agricultural employment declined from about 10 percent of total employment in the mid-1950s to less than 3 percent in the 1990s. Over this same period, employment in goods-producing industries, transportation, and public utilities declined from about 50 percent of nonagricultural employment to about 25 percent, and union membership declined from about 35 percent of private employment to about 10 percent (but increased substantially among government employees). The change in the composition of employment, in turn, is a major cause of both the rapid increase in employment opportunities for women and the decline in union membership.

Changes in the composition of employment, of course, may also affect average compensation, even if the relative compensation among sectors has not changed. The substantial reallocation of employment from agriculture, the goods-producing industries, transportation, and public utilities to the more heterogeneous service sector, however, does not appear to be a major cause of the increased variance of wages (Valletta 1997a). Changes in production techniques that increase the demand for skilled workers appear to be the major cause. Early studies estimated the contribution of technological change only by a process of elimination, but recent direct evidence supports their conclusions (Johnson 1997).

We seem to be at the dawn of a third industrial revolution, one based on the rapid development of digital technology and biotechnology. Applications for U.S. patents, for example, nearly doubled from 1985 to 1995. One important puzzle, however, must be sorted out. The past few decades have witnessed a rapid development of both information technology and biotechnology. From 1974 through 1995, however, the rate of growth of (measured) productivity was unusually low, and the variance of earnings by education increased. If these new technologies are so important, why were they not reflected in the productivity data? Why would new technology increase the variance of wages?

There are several answers to this puzzle. One answer is that our measures of output growth are biased downward for the same reasons that our measures of inflation are biased upward—inadequate measures of the value of new products, quality improvements, and product and outlet substitution. The Boskin Commission, for example, estimated that the consumer price index overstates the inflation rate by about one percentage point. Although this estimate has been the subject of some dispute, there is widespread agreement among economists that inflation has been overstated to some extent, which means that the real earnings of Americans have been rising faster than reported by the current statistics and that low-income workers in particular may not be suffering as large an erosion in their real earnings as has been commonly believed.

One issue that the Boskin Commission did not address is whether the inflation bias has increased over time, which some observers believe has occurred. If, however, the bias has been roughly constant over the past few decades, actual productivity growth has been higher than the measured rate but has declined by the same amount. In any case, whether or not the real earnings of low-skill workers have increased or declined, the variance of earnings has increased.

A more comprehensive answer is that slower growth of measured productivity and a higher variance of earnings may be characteristic of the early stages of a major technological change. Careful studies of the industrial revolutions in Britain and the United States find that measured productivity growth declined and the variance of earnings increased for the first twenty to forty years after the introduction of the steam engine and, later, electrical power (Greenwood 1997). Only later did major productivity benefits show up as firms and individuals learned how to use the new technologies to make old things in new ways and to come up with new things entirely. To be sure, the microprocessor has been with us for a quarter century, but firms and individuals are still learning to adapt to it, and most of its benefits probably lie in the future.

The two hypotheses that best fit this evidence have interesting implications for understanding recent experience: measured output understates actual output because it does not include the substantial investment involved in learning how to use the new technology. Educated workers have an advantage in implementing new technology, but the relative demand for educated workers will decline as the stock of learning increases. All of this suggests that measured U.S. productivity growth should increase and the variance of earnings should decline, as indeed has happened in the past few years. The puzzling combination of current economic conditions may be a basis for optimism that these recent conditions will continue.

Over the past twenty-five years, the share of international trade in U.S. gross domestic product (GDP) roughly doubled. This has led many commentators, including some economists, to conclude that the increased variance of wages may be a consequence of increased international trade. And this relation is quite plausible. Increased trade increases the demand for high-skill labor that is more abundant in the United States than in the rest of the world and increases the effective supply of low-skill labor that is more abundant in the rest of the world than in the United States. The coincident increase in the variance of wages in the United States and the increase in unemployment in Europe suggests that increased international trade may cause problems for low-skill workers in high-wage countries, with the nature of these problems depending on the characteristics of each labor market.

Most trade economists tend to minimize the effect of trade on the increased variance of wages. As evidence, they note that most low-skill labor works in service sectors not directly affected by trade, that the relative prices of low-skill-intensive goods have declined only slightly, and that the relative employment of high-skill labor has increased in most sectors. At most, trade economists attribute only 10 to 20 percent of the increase of wage variance to increased trade. In contrast, some labor economists claim that the increase in imports of manufactured goods from low-wage countries has also induced part of the technological change in the traded goods sector, has indirectly reduced wages in other sectors, and may explain 50 to 100 percent of the increase of wage variance.

Both of these groups, however, reject protectionism in favor of skill development as the appropriate policy response. This issue is complex and contentious and is unlikely to be resolved soon, either among economists or in the policy community. For the moment, I share the judgment of Richard Freeman, who, summarizing a symposium on income inequality and trade, concludes, "trade matters, but it is neither all that matters nor the primary cause of observed changes" (Freeman 1995, 30).

A related and similarly contentious issue is the increase in immigration. Again, it is plausible that the increase in immigration, mostly from low-wage countries, may have reduced the real wages of low-skill labor in the United States. A recent survey of the empirical studies on this issue, however, concludes, "The weight of the empirical evidence is that immigration to the United States has not contributed much to reducing wages for low-skill native workers nor to changes in overall wage inequality" (Topel 1997, 5).

A neglected dimension of the plausible causes of the increased variance of wages is the change in the job-related skills and attitudes at any level of education. The available data on high school students who aspire to college are very disturbing. The average composite Scholastic Aptitude Test score declined substantially from the mid-1960s to 1980 and has since recovered only slightly. In 1995, 41 percent of freshmen at public two-year colleges and 22 percent of freshmen at public four-year colleges were required to take at least one remedial course. Apparently, a high school degree does not represent an adequate preparation for college.

Less is known about the change in job skills of those who do not attend college, but the indirect evidence is even more disturbing. A study of the wage variance among countries in the Organization for Economic Cooperation and Development (OECD) observed that the skills of those at the bottom of the U.S. wage distribution are lower than those of similar workers in Europe (Blau and Kahn 1996). The dramatic change in family structure clearly has contributed to a number of problems, including poor school performance, employment problems, and crime. From 1960 through 1995, for example, the percentage of births to single mothers increased from 2 to 25 percent among whites and from 22 to 70 percent among blacks. Many job skills are learned on-the-job, but the employment rate for young black males declined from 52 percent in 1954 to 28 percent in 1998. These demographic and employment trends have not yet been reversed and are likely to cast a shadow on the potential wages of low-skill workers for many years. An absolute reduction in job-related skills must explain some of the decline in the real wages of low-skill workers, although, to my knowledge, no direct estimate of this effect has been made.

One related development during this period merits more attention. Although the variance of wages by skill level increased, the variance of wages by sex and race declined. The wage differential between men and women fell from 37 percent in 1984 to 24 percent in 1995. At the same time, the wage gap narrowed from 27 to 18 percent, respectively, for white and black males and from 9 to 6 percent, respectively, for white and black females (Lerman 1997). In that sense, the American wage structure has become more meritocratic—more a function of acquired skills and less a function of conditions of one's birth.

Finally, changes in labor market institutions may explain part of the increased variance of wages. Three conditions have been studied: the decline in the percentage of private employees covered by union contracts, the decline in the real minimum wage, and the substantial reduction of economic regulation. One recent study attributes about one-third of the increase in the variance of wages during the 1980s to these conditions—with deunionization an important condition for men, the decline in the real minimum wage more important for women, and no significant effect of the reduction of economic regulation (Fortin and Lemieux 1997). One caveat is that this study ignores the employment effects of lower unionism and lower real minimum wages. Total employment increased rapidly during these years, especially for women, so the effect of these conditions on the variance of earnings is likely to be smaller than the effect on the variance of wage rates.

What Should Be Done About These Developments? A Personal Perspective

My strongest inclination is to reject the European model for the U.S. labor market. Although conditions differ somewhat among the European countries, the most important common characteristics of the European labor market are centralized wage-setting processes, government restrictions on firing, and relatively generous unemployment benefits of extended duration. The first characteristic leads to a compression of wages at the bottom of the wage distribution, increasing the lowest wages relative to the median wage; this increases the earnings of those employed, reduces the incentive of workers to improve their skills, and reduces the incentive of employers to hire the least skilled. The restrictions on firing also reduce the incentive to hire, transforming labor from a variable input into a capital input. The third characteristic reduces the incentive of the unemployed to find another job. The combination of these characteristics leads to low employment growth, high unemployment rates, unusually high long-term unemployment rates, and high government expenditures for unemployment and welfare. Table 3.1 summarizes these conditions for the major European countries and the United States.

Since 1995 employment conditions in Europe and the United States have continued to diverge. As of August 1999, the standardized unemployment rate was 9.2 percent in OECD Europe and only 4.2 percent in the United States. European labor policies have reduced the variance of wages in the bottom half of the wage distribution, but only at a great cost in employment conditions. I doubt that many Americans would prefer this combination of wage and employment conditions.

In that case, what, if anything, should be done about the increased variance of wages in the United States? There is a reasonable case that nothing should be done. People do not have a property right to the *value* of their skills and other assets. Moreover, they have no inherent right to claim a share of the income of other people who may have benefited relatively more from market developments. Any consensus on redistribution must be based on either the ex ante consent of the larger community regarding the rules for redistribution or the ex post consent of those from whom the transfers are made. There is a reasonable basis for assuming that, "behind the veil of ignorance," most Americans would agree to some rule for redistribution, although the Constitution now provides no authority for such a rule. There is also a reasonable basis for assuming that those who benefit most from life's lottery would agree to some amount of some type of redistribution. One implication of either the contractarian or libertarian perspective, however, is that transfers should be focused on those near the bottom of the distribution for reasons largely not of their own choosing. This suggests that the proper focus is on the wages of the least skilled, not on the variance of wages. A reduction of the post-tax-and-transfer variance of wages may be an effect of the preferred policy but should not be its goal.

Table 3.1 Employment Conditions in Europe and the United States, 1985 to 1995 (Percentage)

Country	Civilian Employment		Unemployment Rate	
	Rate 1995	Change 1985 to 1995	Rate 1995	Unemployed More Than One Year
France	48.8	3.3	11.7	45.6
Germany[a]	49.7	6.5	6.5	48.3
Italy	41.8	−2.4	12.0	62.9
Spain[b]	44.2	9.4	23.8	56.5
United Kingdom	56.7	6.2	8.8	49.8
United States	62.9	16.5	5.6	9.7

Source: OECD in figures 1997.
[a] Former Federal Republic of Germany only.
[b] Rate in 1994 and change from 1984 to 1994.

Finally, my priority is to remove those government barriers that restrict the opportunities of the least skilled. Such measures have the best prospect of being positive-sum games for all those with the relevant rights.

One of the two most important American domestic policy issues in the next several decades will be a profound reform of the organization of kindergarten through twelfth-grade schooling. (The other major issue, the transition to a sustainable retirement income and health insurance program, must be faced by most of the OECD countries.) A growing concern about the quality of U.S. public schooling led to the creation of numerous official commissions, most notably summarized by a 1983 report, *A Nation at Risk:* "The educational foundations of our society are presently being eroded by a rising tide of mediocrity that threatens our very future as a Nation and a people" (National Commission on Excellence in Education 1983, 63). These commissions promoted a laundry list of reforms in the public school systems that are still under way, for the most part with little net benefit. For fifty years, real spending per student in the public schools has increased nearly 40 percent a decade, but most measures of student performance, especially for students in inner-city public schools, are lower now than in the mid-1960s.

In parallel with these commissions, fortunately, a number of scholars completed careful studies of the comparative performance of students in public and private schools, the most important of which was by James Coleman and his colleagues (Coleman, Hoffer, and Kilgore 1982). All of the comparative studies found that the cost per student is substantially smaller in Catholic schools than in public schools in the same area. The most controversial of the Coleman findings is that the performance of students from disadvantaged backgrounds is substantially higher in

Catholic high schools than in inner-city public high schools. The most counterintuitive of the Coleman findings is that Catholic schools are more integrated by race than the characteristic public school that draws students only from the local area.

The Coleman study provoked a furious response from the educational community, but its primary conclusions have been confirmed by the broader body of "effective schools research" and have now become conventional wisdom. Building on this research, an influential 1990 book by two Brookings scholars made the case for a general system of tax-financed vouchers in which "Schools would be legally autonomous: free to govern themselves as they want, specify their own goals and methods, design their own organizations, select their own student bodies, and make their own personnel decisions. Parents and students would be legally empowered to choose alternative schools, aided by institutions designed to promote active involvement, well-informed decisions, and fair treatment" (Chubb and Moe 1990, 226). Since that time, a growing number of scholars and officials have endorsed some form of education voucher system.

And small tax-financed voucher programs are now under way in Milwaukee and Cleveland. In Milwaukee, about 1,500 children from low-income families get about $4,700 each to attend private secular schools, a program initiated in 1991. In Cleveland, about 1,300 children receive vouchers of up to $2,500 each to attend either secular or religious schools, a program initiated in 1996. The early experience led the state legislatures in both Wisconsin and Ohio to expand these programs, but the expansion has been delayed pending resolution of constitutional challenges initiated by the teachers' unions.

Both of these programs have been subject to careful testing. In Milwaukee, the average voucher student had reading scores five percentage points higher in the fourth year than public school students with similar backgrounds and had math scores twelve percentage points higher. A study of two schools in the Cleveland program found average gains in the first year of five percentage points on reading tests and fifteen percentage points on math tests (Peterson and Hassel 1998). Moreover, a recent study of the broader experience with school competition indicates that "competition from private schools does not have a significant effect on public school spending per pupil [and] that if private schools in an area receive sufficient resources to subsidize each student's tuition by 1,000 dollars, then the achievement of public school students is higher, regardless of whether it is measured by test scores, ultimate educational attainment, or wages" (Hoxby 1998, 8).

A related development has been the rapid growth of privately financed school voucher programs for children of low-income families. These programs characteristically finance half or more of the tuition at private schools for children of poor households. In 1998 there were thirty-six such programs with more than 12,000 students enrolled and many times that number on waiting lists. In June 1998 two leading businessmen offered a challenge grant of $100 million to expand these programs by about 50,000 students. There has yet to be an evaluation of these private voucher programs other than the testimony of many grateful parents.

The barriers to tax-financed voucher programs may be reduced soon. In June 1998 the Wisconsin Supreme Court approved a plan to expand the Milwaukee voucher program to include church-affiliated schools, but this decision will surely be appealed. On that same day, Congress approved a tax-free education savings account that parents could have used for private school tuition if the bill had not been vetoed. My judgment is that school choice will expand quickly and will prove to be the most effective policy to improve the quality of elementary and secondary schooling and to restore the inner city.

Vocational Training and the Transition from School to Work

In the United States the transition from school to work has little structure and is not very effective, but there is little agreement on what might work better. Training systems based on the German model might seem to be an attractive alternative; in the countries that use this system, a majority of those ages sixteen through nineteen spend most of the work week in work site training, augmented by one or two days of related school studies. In Germany, more than 20 percent of employers participate in this system, and about 60 percent of young people choose their vocation and their first job based on these apprenticeships. American educators and employers, however, both reject the German model, reflecting a concern about the early tracking and narrow vocational specialties that characterize this system. A recent report by an employers group, for example, recommends a combination of improved general academic standards, the development of interactive skills based on actual or simulated work experience, and a network of intermediary organizations that link schools and employers, but the report acknowledges that the limited experience with this model is not encouraging (Committee for Economic Development 1998). My guess is that the American school-to-work transition process will continue to be unsatisfactory. The only effective alternatives seem to be either better general academic training or earlier tracking to work-based vocational training.

American employers, again, prefer employees with better general academic skills to those with school-based vocational training. According to a recent survey, the proportion of American businesses providing remedial basic education for employees increased from 18 percent in 1984 to 43 percent in 1995; these costs could be saved if school performance were better (Smith 1996). More specific vocational training is best provided on-the-job, and American businesses would provide more vocational training if not for the unusual turnover among young workers. The average American worker has held more than seven jobs by age twenty-nine. The major alternative policies to induce a more optimal amount of vocational training are tax-financed training programs and some form of indenture contract to reduce turnover. Tax credits and wage subsidies, however, have not proved to be an efficient policy for encouraging employers to participate in training programs (Office of Technology Assessment 1995).

And the many government training programs for low-skill workers, except for adult women, also have a discouraging record (Friedlander, Greenberg, and Robins 1997). For much of American history, most young employees, especially immigrants, worked under an indenture contract for a period until their employers recouped the costs of transportation and training. This practice has largely disappeared, except for expensive specialized military and medical training, maybe because an employee who chafes at the indenture is not worth maintaining, maybe because the courts will no longer enforce an indenture contract. In any case, the once-common arrangement for providing vocational training is no longer acceptable, the many new experiments with tax-financed training have not been effective, and the losers have been those who leave school without either good academic or work skills. On this issue, I have yet to read a creative proposal.

Opportunities for the Least Skilled

Many government policies affect the employment and earnings opportunities of the least skilled. The most important of these is the earned income tax credit (EITC), a federal program that augments the earnings of workers in low-income households. For a household with two or more children, in 1996 this program subsidized earnings at a 40 percent rate up to an annual income of $8,890 and phased out this subsidy at a 21 percent rate on incomes above $11,610. This program has a high participation rate, low administrative costs, an undesirably high rate of overclaims, and an annual budget cost of about $28 billion. It has been especially effective in helping women substitute work for welfare. Over the phaseout range, however, many EITC recipients face a combined marginal tax rate of more than 50 percent—the sum of the phaseout rates for EITC and food stamps, the payroll tax rate, and the federal and state income tax rates—a rate that significantly reduces work, especially by secondary workers in low-to-middle-income households. The cost of this program has increased rapidly and the political support has narrowed, but the EITC should be considered an essential component of welfare reform.

Other measures that would increase the opportunities for low-skill workers include the repeal or rejection of government barriers to work. A repeal of the minimum wage should be at the top of the list. The misleading rationale and tortured evidence for the minimum wage no longer merit serious attention. An increase in the minimum wage would significantly reduce the legal employment of the least-skilled workers, probably by about 0.2 times the percentage increase in the real minimum wage, and most of the benefits of the wage increase would accrue to secondary workers in nonpoor households. For the same reason, the government should reject the recurrent proposals for mandates on employers to provide health insurance, family leave, and other benefits that would disproportionately increase the cost of hiring the least-skilled workers. One local government measure that would especially help the more entrepreneurial of low-skill workers would be to repeal the limits on the number of taxicabs and street vendors and on the licensing of certain occupations such as barbers and beauticians.

Labor Law

Most of my remaining suggestions bear on what policies should *not* be approved in the name of good jobs and good wages. Labor law is a good place to start. For the most part, the U.S. labor market works very well. Over the past several decades, however, a gradual erosion of the "employment at will" doctrine, largely by state courts, has contributed to significant differences in employment growth by state. In effect, this doctrine set the default rule on firing; in the absence of an explicit labor contract, employers were presumed to have the right to fire any employee without cause and without notice. In effect, the accumulation of exceptions to this doctrine substituted a state-designed labor contract for the pattern of explicit and implicit private employment arrangements and increased the expected cost of hiring new employees. State legislators should evaluate the effects of these exceptions on labor market conditions in their state.

One recent development in federal labor law merits attention. Over the past several years, the National Labor Relations Board has declared that "quality circles" in several nonunion firms are in fact company unions and therefore illegal under the Wagner Act. (Quality circles are problem-solving work teams focused on improving quality or productivity.) This represents an artificial restriction on a structure of work relations that has proved both productive and popular in other firms. These decisions should be reversed. At the same time, it is important to reject the recurrent proposals to mandate or subsidize changes in the structure of work relations. Decision sharing or profit sharing may increase productivity in some firms, but there is no reason to expect the government to have superior information about these effects or for a specific structure to be best for all firms.

Macroeconomic Policy

The record of the past forty years should be sufficient evidence of a *positive* relation between unemployment and inflation in the long term. The primary policy implication of the new macroeconomics is that monetary policy should be designed to stabilize a path of aggregate demand such that the expected inflation rate is about zero. Fiscal policy should be designed for long-term objectives, not as an instrument of discretionary macroeconomic policy.

Social Policies

A range of social policies could have important effects on the number and economic prospects of low-skill workers. The most important social policy objective, I suggest, would be to reduce the number of births to single mothers—a condition that now contributes to low school performance, employment problems, and a high crime rate; I have yet to read a creative proposal to address this condition. Young workers, especially blacks, and two-worker households should expect a very low return from social security; allowing workers to divert most of their payroll tax to personal retirement accounts would especially benefit these groups. Social services to low-wage workers, such as child care, should be provided, if at all, by a tax-financed means-tested subsidy, not by mandates on employers.

Taxes

Several changes to the federal income tax should also be considered. Increasing the personal exemption would sharply reduce the marginal tax rate faced by those with wages in the phaseout range for the EITC and other benefits. The federal income tax, like the social security retirement program, is also biased against the two-worker household, by making the marginal tax rate of the second worker dependent on the income of the first worker; broadening the 15 percent tax bracket may be the most efficient way to reduce this bias. The tax treatment of health insurance is still biased against the self-employed, permitting a deduction of only 40 percent of the premiums in 1997, with this deduction scheduled to increase to 80 percent by 2006. A broader reform would be necessary to provide equal tax treatment of the self-employed and employees not covered by an employer plan. In general, these tax changes would be most important for those trying to move up into the middle class.

A more general tax reform would be necessary to reduce the severe bias against saving and investment and the misallocative effects of a complex tax base and multiple tax rates.

Trade and Immigration

Finally, a growing chorus of commentators has promised to protect American workers against increased international trade, investment, and immigration. So far, as long as total employment is growing, there has been little popular response to this noisy crowd. This group, however, represents a potentially harmful coalition of the populist left and right when the U.S. economy next turns down. The policies proposed by this group to limit international trade and investment should be strongly rejected in favor, if necessary, of measures to assist those workers who are specifically threatened by the global economy. Similarly, proposals to restrict immigration should be rejected in favor, if necessary, of an increase in the share of skilled workers in the total immigration quotas.

Conclusions

In general, the American labor market works very well—with a low unemployment rate, a rapid reallocation of labor in response to changes in demand and supply, and compensation that is closely related to productivity. Over the past several decades, however, the outcomes of the U.S. labor market reflected two major new conditions: from 1974 through 1995 the growth of (measured) productivity and average real compensation were unusually low, and the level of real compensation and, probably, the skills of the least-skilled workers declined. The primary causes of these two conditions are not fully understood, but both conditions can be reduced or alleviated by identifiable changes in public policies. We need both a broader understanding of the strengths of the U.S. labor market and a broader consensus for the policy changes that would improve the outcomes of this market.

= Chapter 4 =

Enhancing the Opportunities, Skills, and Security of American Workers

WAGES were distributed much less equally among U.S. workers in 1998 than they were in the late 1970s. In this chapter I discuss the implications of that change for workers and for the social polity of the United States more generally. I also critically review the various policy options that are available for responding to rising inequality in the labor market.

A Quick Review of the Facts

Chapter 1 of this volume reviews the facts about rising wage inequality, but it may be useful to revisit some of the key trends that underlie much of the policy discussion. Wage inequality began to rise around 1979. In particular, wages among low-wage workers fell in inflation-adjusted terms, while wages among higher-wage workers rose rapidly. This pattern is in sharp contrast to the pattern in other industrial countries, which experienced rises in wage inequality over this time period. Only in the United States did rising inequality mean actual declines in real wages at the bottom of the distribution; in other countries, wages at the bottom were stagnant or rising more slowly than wages at the top.

Although much of the discussion has focused on rising inequality between less-skilled and more-skilled workers, only about half of the increase in inequality is due to shifts among workers by skill group. Rises in inequality are also visible among workers with similar skill levels; that is to say, the returns to work have become more dispersed, even within skill, age, and occupation groups. Differences across male and female workers are also interesting. The largest wage declines have been experienced by less-skilled men. In contrast, less-skilled women show only modest or no decline, although less-skilled women continue to earn substantially less than less-skilled men. Both more-skilled men and more-skilled women have experienced sharp wage increases.

These relative changes—by gender and within skill group—suggest that the underlying causes of these changes must be complex. They are not spread equally across the economy, but affect the industries and occupations of men more than those of women. They are also related to more nuanced differences in skill and ability than aggregate measures of skill (such as years of education) provide. Even within skill groupings, the labor market is distinguishing more sharply between workers (presumably on the basis of productivity-related skills observed by the employer), raising the variance of wages. A growing body of research has investigated the causes of these trends in wage inequality. This work concludes that shifts in labor demand by skill level are the primary cause. In particular, these demand shifts appear to be due to skill-demanding changes in technology (that have increased the demand for more-skilled workers and decreased the demand for less-skilled workers), increasing globalization of the U.S. economy (which has underscored the comparative advantage of college-educated U.S. labor in the world market), and certain institutional changes (such as the ongoing decline in unionization) that have accompanied technological and economic changes.

Finally, these wage changes are highly correlated with changes in other labor market outcomes. In particular, changes in labor force participation have been related to changes in wages in recent years. Among men, the decline in labor force participation is sharpest among men who have experienced the largest decline in wages. Similarly, the largest increase in labor force participation among women over the past ten to twenty years has been among college-educated married women, whose wage opportunities have increased the most. The relationship between changes in wages and changes in labor force participation indicates how wage changes can fundamentally alter behavior. Although the shifts in labor force participation are the clearest and best documented, observers have suggested that these wage changes also may be related to increases in single motherhood, changes in criminal activity, and changes in welfare caseloads.

Why Should We Care?

This section discusses four major reasons why widening wage inequality is a serious problem confronting the United States and why it demands public policy interventions. I close with a comment about the extent to which the problem is inequality versus deteriorating economic status among less-skilled workers.

A Signal of Productivity Problems

The decline in wages (and the related decline in demand) for less-skilled workers is a signal that this segment of the labor force is becoming increasingly less competitive. This almost surely indicates a basic productivity problem. Either these workers have received the wrong education (they are blacksmiths in a world of automobiles), or they have received too little education (they are ditch diggers in a world of computer operators). The decline in wages for these less-productive workers should serve as a market signal inducing current and future workers to respond to changes in demand by increasing their skill levels and raising their productivity.

Allowing the labor market to adjust to these changes by itself will be a very slow process. As a result, the "market signal" is not adequate, and there are reasons to engage in explicit policy measures that either cushion individuals from these changes or help them respond more rapidly. Most notably, many workers who have left school (are over the age of twenty to twenty-five) find it difficult to change their skill level substantially. This suggests that current twenty-five-year-old high school dropouts are likely to be in the labor market for the next forty years at about their current level of productivity. If demand for their skills continues to decline, they may find it difficult to do anything that would substantially change the wages they can command in the labor market.

The slow pace at which the labor market clears, given forty-five-year work lives and the difficulty of obtaining substantial new training or retraining at older ages, is one reason to argue for a public policy response to rising wage inequality. We have to worry about today's displaced forty-year-old worker or today's twenty-five-year-old high school dropout because these workers are likely to continue to be in the labor market for many years to come, facing declining earnings opportunities.

A further reason why the labor market responds only slowly to changes in relative wages is that there appears to be an enormous lack of information among adolescents and children about their long-term labor market opportunities. Some studies find that teenagers substantially misestimate the returns to various skill investments. This argues for policies that increase the level and flow of information to adolescents, helping them to assess the value of schooling.

These informational problems may be due to more than a simple lack of good high school vocational counseling. For instance, at least some teenagers may fail to invest in skills because of institutional problems in their local school system. This may be particularly true in some of our urban schools where student resources are limited, teachers receive little support, and violence is commonplace. Similar problems may occur if family or neighborhood difficulties limit the structure of information available to children about future life options or do not support even those children who express the ambition for further training. In these cases, the market signal may not get through, and there may be a need to try and fix these institutional and structural problems in order for children to be able to hear and respond to the message about the importance of education.

In short, labor markets may be very slow to adjust to market signals by themselves. Certain groups of workers in particular may have difficulty substantially raising their productivity once they leave school, and others may not receive the market signals early enough for those signals to influence their training decisions. Because labor markets are so sticky and some workers are unable to hear or respond well to market signals, there is a reason to intervene more actively in ways that help workers learn and respond more quickly.

Declining Well-Being

These wage changes—particularly the wage declines among less-skilled workers—may have serious effects on the well-being of individuals and families. Men and women who earn less are less able to support their families. This can result in an increased incidence of poverty and low income. For instance, research suggests that rises in wage inequality prevented the poverty rate from falling as fast in the economic expansion of the 1980s as it did during the expansion of the 1960s. Other research indicates that the rise in the use of public assistance among two-parent families in the late 1980s and early 1990s was at least partly the result of declining relative wages among less-skilled workers.

These changes in earnings can have a host of other effects as well. They are correlated with changes in labor force participation and are a key reason why less-skilled men are reducing their involvement in the labor market. Not only does this reduce their income, but it also detaches these individuals from one of their primary ties to society—mainstream employment—and may result in greater underground employment or crime. This can also result in changes in family structure. For instance, one theory about the rise in single parenting is that deteriorating male wages have made men less willing to marry and women less willing to marry these men.

Among married-couple families, women's earnings are providing a growing share of family income. Some of this reflects the increase in labor market opportunities available to women. But some of it also reflects women's response to their husband's falling earnings and declining labor market involvement. Family incomes have not widened as much as individual earnings, largely because second and third workers in families have made up for some of the earnings losses of individuals. But this means that the adults in families headed by lower-wage workers may be working more hours without any real income gain. Most economists would judge this a clear loss in family well-being.

Finally, even if one is not concerned about reductions in income among today's adults, one might be concerned about the effect of income losses on today's children. All analysts agree that children growing up in poor households are at greater risk of poor health, poor school achievement, and other outcomes that limit future earnings opportunities. There is more disagreement about the extent to which these differences are due to income as opposed to other unmeasured differences between poor and nonpoor families. Most research concludes that family income plays an important role in child outcomes, however, and this should increase our concern about economic changes that may reduce income among low-income families with children.

The social and personal cost of these changes in family well-being are a major reason why it may not be enough just to let the market function as inequality rises. The social costs of greater child poverty or higher crime rates can be substantial. Even though it may "mute" the market signal somewhat, these issues of well-being provide a strong reason to subsidize wages or otherwise cushion individuals and families from some of the worst effects of these wage changes.

Devaluing Employment

Our society places a very high value on employment. Indeed, our economy is structured so that employment of at least one family member is typically necessary for adequate economic survival. Although we provide public assistance programs to those who cannot work, we generally want those who can work to do so. Nowhere is this more apparent than in reforms in public assistance programs over the past decade. A series of welfare reform bills have increasingly defined single mothers, including single mothers with young children, as able to work, in sharp contrast to earlier decades when public assistance was designed explicitly to keep mothers with children at home.

Declines in wages devalue work and weaken the social message that employment demonstrates personal responsibility and makes an important contribution to society. This is not a message we want to weaken, particularly at a time when we are trying to encourage even more low-wage women to enter the labor force than ever before. Among those who can work, employment is a superior outcome to the alternatives, such as public assistance or underground economic activity. This also provides a reason to design policy interventions that offset the effects of wage declines. (I believe that this is one of the reasons why so many industrial societies enact minimum-wage laws. These laws explicitly value employment by helping to assure that work provides economic sufficiency.)

Lessening Civic Cohesion

Behind the individual effects of these wage changes, there may also be a larger social and political effect. With rising wage inequality, the economic experiences of working Americans are becoming increasingly diverse. For some workers, the past ten years have been one of the best decades ever. For others, they constituted a very difficult economic period. These differences in economic reality can seriously erode the potential for holding a common national conversation around key policy and social issues. For instance, the economic instability experienced by less-skilled workers has been identified as at least one possible cause of hostility against racial minorities and immigrants. It is often considered a reason behind the enormous gap in perceptions between the supporters and the opponents of more open trade policy. Others believe that the economic discontent of certain subgroups of Americans has made possible the emergence of candidates, such as Ross Perot, who teach that existing institutions should be distrusted and preach the need for radical change. In short, growing divergence in economic reality among different groups may lead to growing divergence of opinion about current political and social issues, reducing civic discourse throughout society.

Is the Problem Inequality or Deteriorating Wages Among the Least Skilled?

This section has provided a number of arguments about why we should care about the impact of rising wage inequality. With these arguments in mind, it is worth commenting on issues of inequality versus issues of well-being among the least skilled. Most of the problems relate to the decline (or, among women, the stagnation) of wages among low-wage workers. It is possible to agree that such wage declines are problematic without agreeing that rising inequality is, per se, a problem. I have said little about the upper end of the wage distribution, where wages are rising rapidly.

For instance, I believe that rising wage inequality is particularly problematic when it occurs via wage declines (or even wage stagnation) among some groups and significant wage increases among other groups. This situation creates a particularly difficult environment in which some groups "win" and other groups "lose" and feeds most strongly into the negative social effects of devaluing the work of one group relative to that of another and creating social and political fault lines within society. These effects would operate even in an environment where inequality was rising but everyone was experiencing wage increases (and hence even in this situation I would argue that rising inequality would be somewhat problematic), but the negative effects would be much more muted by the general increase in well-being experienced by all workers.

What Should We Do?

There are many possible policy responses to address the recent problems connected to rising wage inequality. This section reviews possible areas of response and critically comments on the most promising directions within each area.

Improved Education

Given a growing body of evidence suggesting that these changes in wages are induced by changes in the relative demand for more- and less-skilled workers, the only long-run solution is to raise the educational skills and productivity of less-skilled workers as they enter the workforce. This means achieving declines in high school dropout rates, improvements in school achievement, and increases in the share of workers who pursue training after high school. In particular, if we are most worried about the least skilled, educational reform efforts should focus on bringing up the bottom.

This means focusing on improving school districts where dropout rates are highest, which are typically center-city school districts and rural school districts. One problem faced by these schools is the lack of effective parental support for children in school (such as helping with homework, paying attention to how kids are doing in school, and communicating the importance of schooling). If this were the whole problem, reform efforts would be extremely difficult. But it is also clear that many of these school districts also have serious institutional problems and provide inadequate resources for their students.

A host of specific reform programs have been proposed to improve urban schools. In specific schools, a number of these reform efforts have shown positive effects. My own reading of the evidence is that the details of how reform is designed matters less than that it contains some specific elements. In particular, reforms must be systemwide. The recent radical restructuring of the authority structure within the Chicago public schools was the only way to provide authority to close schools, to fire certain teachers, and to raise promotional standards. Small reforms aimed at school-by-school efforts ended up being swamped by the larger institutional problems within the entire district. Some people suggest that urban school districts are typically too large to function effectively and even propose dividing cities into a set of smaller school districts.

In addition, reforms aimed at increasing achievement and skill preparation have to start at the earliest ages. Too often, programs designed to prevent dropping out or teen pregnancy exist only in the high schools. Instead, programs targeted to at-risk students should start in elementary and middle schools. Such programs should also be coordinated across the grades, so that students receive consistent encouragement.

A number of specific school reform efforts deserve special comment because they have received so much attention. A host of public-private partnerships have emerged in recent years, as corporations "adopt" specific schools and provide enriched programs or as individuals or organizations "adopt" classes and promise them assistance in preparing for college. In general, these efforts are laudatory, although they need to be sustained over time. In addition, when they focus only on individual schools or classes, their effects may be offset by larger institutional problems within the entire school district. Such partnerships surely are not going to "solve" our educational problems, but they increase the resources and attention focused on at-risk students in helpful ways.

School-to-work transition programs also have been much discussed in recent years. Such programs aim to connect at-risk students more directly to the labor market by providing them with direct internship experiences, by relating their educational curriculum directly to work skills, and by creating an environment in which educational performance is correlated more strongly with work outcomes on graduation. Like public-private partnerships, such efforts are moving in the right direction. Forthcoming evaluations of different school-to-work programs will soon provide us with a better sense of which particular approaches seem to be most effective.

Probably the biggest and most controversial proposal for school reform involves moving to some sort of voucher or choice system, allowing parents to select their child's school (and potentially even funding attendance at private schools). The issues involved in voucher proposals are complex and impossible to discuss well in a few sentences.

In general, I believe that increasing choice within school districts can be a very good thing. Indeed, almost all major urban school districts have created magnet schools or enacted other reforms that allow children who are doing well to self-select into special enriched programs. Such efforts assure that good students will receive the attention they deserve and often function to keep middle-class families in the public schools. However, there is little evidence that such programs have helped to bring up the bottom; in fact, at least some critics have claimed that they segregate the poorer students in even less-adequate schools by drawing resources away to the magnet schools. My concern about more widespread voucher programs echoes some of these concerns. Even though I suspect that vouchers would improve outcomes for students at the top of the ability distribution or those whose parents are most attentive to educational issues, I would be reluctant to engage in a major voucher reform without some assurances that the students who are least able or whose parents pay the least attention will not end up ghettoized in schools that are just as bad as or worse than today's schools.

This is an area where we need more demonstration research. It is difficult to predict the effects of such a major reform with the limited evidence currently available. (Most opponents or supporters of vouchers tend to badly over-interpret the limited amount of evidence available in ways that support their point of view.) I have come to believe that the problems with some of our public school districts are so extensive that I am willing to support experimentation with the type of major restructuring that vouchers would produce. But I would not want to implement such programs across-the-board without a better understanding of their effects, particularly on the students most at risk.

Improving education is a huge topic, which this chapter can touch on only briefly. Let me simply underscore that this is probably the most important issue in the long run for those who are concerned with the decreasing demand for less-skilled workers. We need to permanently raise the skill level of the bottom end of our wage distribution; this is the only way to assure that future generations will not face the sort of wage problems experienced by this generation.

Enhanced Training

If education reforms focus on tomorrow's workers, the next policy area of concern is training and productivity-enhancing activities aimed at today's workers, many of whom will be in the labor force for many years to come. The evidence here is not encouraging. Very few workers substantially raise their skill levels after their mid-twenties.

Publicly provided job training programs for low-skill workers appear to have positive but quite modest effects. For instance, a recent evaluation of the Job Training Partnership Act (JTPA)—the primary training program for the least skilled—suggests that the act raises annual wages among both men and women between $200 and $600 a year for some period of time after training is completed. JTPA programs appear to have no positive effects on teens. As James Heckman has noted, it is impossible to think that public job training programs could possibly reverse the impact of widening wage inequality among less-skilled workers. The effects simply are too small.

The area where we have the most experience and have achieved the greatest success with public job training is among public assistance recipients (primarily single mothers). This group, which often has limited job experience, appears to benefit from even quite short-term job placement and work skills programs. Even these effects, however, are relatively modest. The highest recorded earnings gain in any evaluation is around $1,000 a year, with most evaluations showing smaller effects. In addition, these effects erode after several years.

Public sector training programs will not solve the problem of declining wages among less-skilled workers. They are important, however, as a way to help long-term unemployed or nonworking persons move into employment and as a way to implement the recent welfare-to-work reforms.

Publicly funded training need not imply publicly provided training. Indeed, in the welfare-to-work area a whole host of intermediary organizations have sprung up to provide training to public assistance recipients in lieu of publicly run programs. Although there is little hard research evidence on these intermediaries, the anecdotal evidence suggests that they have (at least in some cases) been quite effective. They are able to concentrate entirely on the training and placement function. Those that appear to be most effective are particularly good at developing connections with the host of private sector employers in the region and at following through with their clients and providing ongoing support even after job placement occurs.

Of course, such training could also be provided by the private sector. The current strong economy has increased the incentives for private employers to train workers to fill positions where labor is scarce. The willingness of private sector employers to hire welfare recipients and to participate in welfare-to-work efforts is at least partly a result of the labor shortages that occur when unemployment is extremely low. It may be difficult for private employers to provide certain types of job training, however. Some potential trainees in welfare-to-work programs have little past labor market experience and need counseling on basic work skills, such as timeliness, grooming, or interactions with fellow employees. Many private sector employers have difficulty providing the type of support necessary to do this sort of counseling effectively, particularly if other newly hired workers in similar jobs are not receiving such training. These problems suggest to me that, although the private sector should be closely involved in the design and establishment of public sector training programs, they may not be the appropriate group to provide the initial training.

A key issue related to training is job progression over time among less-skilled workers. Although many training programs focus largely on placing individuals in jobs, they often pay little attention to the opportunity (or lack of opportunity) for low-wage workers to increase their wages over time. Research is extremely limited in this area. We know that wage growth with experience is more limited among the less skilled than the more skilled, particularly among less-skilled women. We also know that the primary way in which workers raise their wages is by changing jobs; hence, starting work in a low-wage job with little prospect of advancement may not be a problem if the worker can move into an alternative job that pays higher wages. (One of the advantages of unionized jobs has historically been that they offer less-skilled workers the opportunity to earn greater increases in pay without having to change jobs.) However, there is little research studying the "job ladders" that less-skilled workers have used to improve their wages and work outlook. For instance, certain starting jobs (for instance, in the rapidly growing health care industry) may offer more opportunity for upward advancement through job switches; this is potentially important information for training programs. As the labor market is reconfigured via changes in demand, it will be increasingly important to focus on more than just initial job placement among less-skilled workers entering the labor market and also to be concerned with long-term wage and earnings prospects, particularly for workers who want and need to support families with their earnings.

Expanded Wage Subsidies

We have enacted some very important wage subsidy legislation in the past decade, at least partly in response to declining wages among the less skilled. The combined effects of increases in the earned income tax credit (EITC) and in the minimum wage since 1989 are extremely large and substantially improve the returns to work among low-wage workers in the face of declining or stagnant market wages.

The earned income tax credit has become the largest means-tested program in the United States (outside of medicaid). It provides wage subsidies to low-income workers through the federal tax system, including a

116   A Working Nation

refundable subsidy to workers who do not owe federal taxes. (A small EITC is currently available to workers without children; larger EITC subsidies are only available to parents.) Adjusted for inflation, the maximum subsidy for a mother with two children has increased 210 percent since 1989 to $3,656 a year in 1997. This is a very large subsidy.

Increases in the minimum wage are also a form of wage subsidy in the short run, although, since the minimum wage is paid by the private sector, in the long run minimum-wage workers must increase their productivity as the minimum wage increases. This can occur by firms improving the technology used by minimum-wage workers, improving the management of minimum-wage workers, or replacing these workers with more-skilled workers over time. The minimum wage rose from $3.35 per hour ($4.34 in 1997 dollars) to $5.15 between 1989 and the end of 1997. Adjusting for inflation, this is a 19 percent increase.

A major concern is that the minimum wage might create potential disemployment effects. Particularly as market wages among less-skilled workers are falling, one might be concerned that further increases in the minimum wage will raise unemployment in this population. So far, these effects appear to have been relatively small in the minimum-wage increases of the 1990s. Economists David Card and Alan Krueger have done a major reevaluation of their own earlier (and controversial) research study with improved data, indicating relatively small disemployment effects from the 1990 and 1991 increases. More recently, researchers at the Employment Policy Institute have studied the minimum-wage changes of 1996 and 1997 by replicating past studies of earlier changes using more recent data. They also find relatively small effects.

The combined effects of the changes in the EITC and in the minimum wage on potential earnings among low-wage workers are shown in table 4.1. The table shows the earnings of a single mother with one child and with two children who is working full-time at the minimum wage in 1989 and 1997. The mother of one child experiences a 27 percent increase in her earnings, and the mother of two experiences an astonishing 42 percent increase in her earnings, simply due to the minimum-wage and EITC expansions. In both cases, by 1997 women have earnings that place them above the poverty line.

It is hard to overemphasize the importance of these policy changes. They have occurred at a time when market wages among low-wage workers have been stagnant or declining and have played a major role in offsetting these trends, particularly among single mothers who are more likely than any other group to have both low wages and low incomes. In fact, because wages among the least-skilled women have been largely stagnant rather than declining, these policy changes have substantially

Table 4.1 **Effects of Changing Policy on Earnings of Single Mothers, 1989 and 1997**

Indicator	1989	1997	Percentage Change
Earnings for a single mother (1997 U.S. dollars)			
With one child	9,856	12,510	26.9
With two children	9,856	13,956	41.6
Ratio of earnings to poverty line for a single mother			
With one child	0.89	1.13	n.a.
With two children	0.76	1.08	n.a.

Source: Author's calculations.
Note: Figures are for a single mother working full-time at minimum wage (assuming 2,000 hours of work per year).

increased the returns to work in this population. A growing body of research relates changes in these policies to growth in labor market participation among single mothers with children.

An extremely important policy issue in the near future is to maintain the value of the EITC and to consider further increases in the minimum wage. These policies have done more to offset the problems caused by widening wage inequality than any other approach. Wage subsidies *must* go hand-in-hand with education and training efforts. Simply to subsidize wages alone would mute the market signals telling young workers to stay in school and receive further training.

An alternative to worker-provided wage subsidies, such as the EITC, are firm-provided wage subsidies. Although we have experimented with small programs of this sort in the past, this country has never run a major public employer wage subsidy program. In general, I believe that worker-provided subsidies are probably preferable to employer-provided subsidies for at least three reasons. First, one wants to provide subsidies based on total family income, not individual wages, to avoid subsidizing the large number of low-wage workers who live in middle- or high-income families. Employers do not have information on family earnings, and it is difficult to imagine how an employer-based subsidy could easily take such information into account. Second, employer-based subsidies are likely to have greater problems with worker displacement, where subsidized workers replace unsubsidized workers, or with wage displacement, where employers pay workers less than they would in the absence of the subsidy and use the government subsidy to subsidize their own labor bill. Although some employers might think of the EITC in this way, there is little evidence that this occurs. Employers know little about whether their workers are eligible for the EITC, because they know little about aggregate family income and child support responsibilities. Third, employer subsidies are public in a way that tax refunds are not. There is a greater potential for workers to be stigmatized and stereotyped by their eligibility for employer subsidies in a way that does not occur with private tax filings.

Other Forms of Employment Subsidies

Wage subsidies are not the only form of employment subsidy. Two other types of public subsidies are increasingly important in raising the real compensation available to workers, namely, child care subsidies and health insurance subsidies.

Particularly with the emphasis on helping public assistance recipients enter the labor market, the availability and quality of child care has become an increasingly important policy issue. Women who do not have reliable and dependable child care available to them are not going to be able to hold a stable job. In response to these concerns, federally funded child care subsidies have grown enormously, from less than $200 million in 1990 to $4 billion in 1997. Yet many observers believe that existing dollars are not adequate to fund women who need assistance with child care or worry that the quality of care that many low-wage women are able to purchase is not adequate.

In a nation where health insurance is provided largely as an employer benefit, health insurance subsidies to low-income families are also an employment subsidy. Few low-wage jobs provide health insurance benefits. Since the mid-1980s, the medicaid program has dramatically expanded its coverage of children in poor and near-poor families, so that all low-income children are now covered by medicaid. Too few families, however, appear to be aware of this coverage, and current efforts are trying to expand access. Health insurance among low-income working adults remains a problem, however. This problem has become more acute over time as health costs have climbed far faster than the rate of inflation. Although there has been only a small decline in health insurance coverage among low-wage workers, the economic risks associated with lack of insurance are much greater now than in the past.

Although the issues of both child care and health care are extremely important, they are not uniquely related to widening wage inequality. Even in the absence of widening inequality, welfare reform would raise concerns about child care subsidies, and rising health costs would raise concerns about lack of health insurance coverage. Even though further efforts to improve the availability of both child care and health insurance to low-wage workers will certainly improve their incentives for employment and raise their disposable income from employment, we should be pursuing these goals regardless of changes in relative wages.

Demand-Side Strategies

Demand-side strategies are designed to increase the demand for less-skilled workers. In the current economic environment, they have received little attention; they tend to become more salient in times of high unemployment and sluggish growth. Demand-side policies can range from small, targeted programs (such as a public sector job program for labor market entrants from high-poverty areas) to massive national programs (such as an industrial planning strategy that allocates greater resources to industries that employ greater numbers of less-skilled workers). Although these more radical strategies are simply not within the set of political choices in this country, there are regular calls for some level of demand-side policy, such as greater trade protection for industries that experience competition from low-wage workers abroad.

I am generally not a fan of most demand-side strategies, for all the reasons that economists typically give to oppose such policies. The research suggests that shifts in demand between more- and less-skilled workers are driving much of the rise in wage inequality. Furthermore, these shifts are not unique to the United States; they appear to be occurring in most of our competitor industrial countries. Under these circumstances, trying to override the market by mitigating these shifts in demand is likely to create enormous inefficiencies and to limit the long-term productivity of American firms.

This is particularly true of trade protection proposals that attempt to insulate U.S. companies from international competition. In the short run, this might result in less job reallocation across workers, but in the long run it will result in lower overall employment and income throughout the United States.

Yet, even though I oppose large-scale trade protection policies, it is important to recognize that movement toward greater free trade will result in some industrial and employment dislocation within the United States. This dislocation is perhaps exactly what we need to remain competitive in the long term, but that is small comfort to the displaced workers who permanently lose their job and experience a large loss in earnings. This suggests that some sort of trade adjustment assistance program may be useful for helping dislocated workers and impacted industries adjust to the new economic reality. I do not believe that we fully understand how to run such programs effectively. The current trade adjustment assistance (TAA) program is a good start, but it probably is not as efficiently targeted or as effective as it could be.

I also believe that there is a strong argument for targeted demand-side strategies in certain circumstances. For instance, as we push to place more public assistance recipients in work, some of these women will not be ready for private sector employment. In these circumstances, women may benefit from a time-limited public sector employment program in which they can learn basic work skills and stabilize their life around steady employment, before searching for private sector work. A similar argument can be made for other extremely disadvantaged populations that are not easily moved into private sector employment without some transitional publicly provided employment. (Of course, this need not be employment in the public sector; it could be publicly subsidized employment in any organization that agrees to provide a supportive environment to help someone move into stable employment.)

Similarly, in times of high unemployment, I would also support targeted demand-side measures intended to maintain steady employment among workers in low-income families. This could involve a countercyclical public sector employment program, or it could involve targeted wage subsidies for certain groups of workers in recessions.

The demand-side strategies of which I am most supportive are basically designed to improve the employment prospects of the most disadvantaged workers. I would generally oppose demand-side strategies designed to maintain employment among more-skilled workers, who are exactly the group most able to respond to the market signal that they need to retrain or actively seek work in another industry.

Labor Management Policy and Worker Organization

Widening wage inequality appears to be linked closely to changes in the use and management of labor. In particular, widening inequality among workers with similar education levels in the same industry or occupation suggests that firms are trying to link pay more directly to individual productivity. In addition, these changes have also been linked to the growing use of temporary workers as well as to the decline in traditional unionization. In a world of increased global competition, it has become harder for workers to capture rents (as the economists say), because firms are operating on a narrower margin and must operate as flexibly as possible to respond immediately to their competitors.

This makes me relatively worried about the future of the traditional union movement in the United States. Those unions that were historically most successful in raising pay among their members have existed in industries with some monopoly control over their market (such as the durable manufacturing industries in the United States following World War II). The union give-backs of recent decades were a predictable (and probably necessary) attempt by U.S. firms and workers to remain competitive as their market control faded and competitors abroad became more powerful.

Of course, as particular groups in the labor market become relatively more disadvantaged, the possibility of a resurgent labor movement may grow (although there are few signs of any growth in organized unrest at present). The question is what workers can demand in the future to force some amount of redistribution—similar to that provided by traditional American unions—to less-skilled workers. It is possible, particularly as firms try to operate increasingly flexible workplaces, that the "new" form of worker organization will demand a greater say in the management structure and labor use of the firm, without as large an effect on wages as unions have traditionally had in the past.

The other alternative is that labor unrest or concern over declining wages among the less skilled could lead to new technologies that substantially increase productivity among the least skilled (in contrast to the past fifteen years in which the new technologies seemed to be most beneficial for more-skilled workers). Some observers have suggested that the computer revolution has hardly begun within the workplace and that "smart" machines will increasingly spread their productivity benefits to less-and-less-skilled workers, resulting in a surge in productivity and wages across the earnings distribution.

All of these proposals, however, are no more than dreams of the future. It is hard to foresee how worker organization and management structure might change over time in response to (still unknown) future changes in technology. It is also possible that future changes might lead to a further widening in wage inequality.

The rising use of more temporary help does raise some explicit policy issues. The great majority of workers who are in jobs that are not permanently connected to a firm appear to prefer this form of work. This includes independent contractors, persons working for temporary placement agencies, and on-call workers. For persons who enjoy the challenges of working in a variety of changing work environments, and who have specialized skills that many firms cannot afford to hire full time in-house, such work can be rewarding. A major problem raised by these jobs, however, is that workers become disconnected from the benefits that are typically offered only by firms, including pension benefits, health insurance, disability insurance, and so on.

The best adaptation of institutional structures to such changes has occurred in the area of pensions, where a host of new privately initiated and tax-reduced retirement savings plans are available, making it profitable and easy for individuals to save for retirement even if they do not receive any form of company pension. In contrast, the health insurance market is far less well adapted to these changes in job structure. It is difficult (sometimes impossible) and expensive to buy health insurance as an individual if one is not covered by a company-based plan with widespread risk sharing. Improving the availability of key benefits, such as health insurance or disability insurance, so that workers who are not closely connected with a single firm do not suffer disproportionately is a major policy need in coming years.

Immigration Policy

The research evidence suggests that changes in worker supply and worker demographics have had only a minor effect on widening wage inequality. Perhaps the most concern in this area has focused on the role played by immigrants, whose share of the U.S. population has increased rapidly over the past two decades. The evidence suggests that increased immigration has had (at best) minor effects on wage inequality, although it appears to have caused some movement of less-skilled native workers out of regions with heavy immigration.

The growing immigrant population raises several concerns, however. First, if immigration continues at its current pace, one might expect larger and larger "competition effects" between immigrants and native workers, particularly less-skilled workers. Second, the growth in immigration may over time further emphasize the problems of certain groups of native workers (particularly African American men). If many of today's recent immigrants are able to move up the job and earnings ladder, this could further emphasize how "stuck" some groups are at the bottom of that ladder where wages have deteriorated.

I would be concerned if we were to face the prospect of large and increasing immigrant flows of low-skilled workers in the next decade. This would create a growing group of workers who are on the wrong side of the demand shifts occurring in the labor market. At least under some circumstances, if fully convinced of this problem, I might consider placing some skill restrictions on immigration. However, it is unclear whether today's immigrants will remain "stuck" at the bottom or if they will assimilate over time and climb the job ladder. It may be particularly likely that today's immigrant children will experience greater upward mobility than their parents. Under these circumstances, the costs of restricting immigration (particularly in a nation with a long history of relatively open immigration) may well be greater than the benefits.

More optimistically, I suspect that recent high levels of immigration may provide us with an opportunity to work with renewed interest on the difficult overlapping problems of race and labor market preparation. The increasing presence of immigrants—particularly immigrants who are not white Caucasians—can be an impetus to enforce equal opportunity laws by both race and ethnicity. Similarly, such immigrants provide a further argument for why we need the most effective public schools and the best training programs available. And as we grow used to greater racial diversity, this may also lessen some of the long-simmering racial tensions in the country. In short, the recent relatively high levels of immigration only reinforce some of the policy needs mentioned and may make it easier to win support for them in the long run.

Conclusions

All indications suggest that the recent widening in wage inequality—and especially the decline in demand for less-skilled workers—is unlikely to reverse itself in the near future. In the worst case, it could widen even further if changes in technology and growing global competition continue to benefit more-skilled workers at the expense of less-skilled workers. We are currently in what appears to be an abatement of these effects, but it is too early to judge whether this is simply the short-run result of a tight labor market in an extended economic expansion or a real slowdown in the widening inequality of the past two decades. In any case, the policy issues raised by this widening inequality will not go away in the near future.

My own priority list for policies relating to widening wage inequality include the following:

1. Do everything possible to implement effective school reform, particularly in school districts with high levels of dropouts and low achievement.
2. Maintain the current level of the EITC and the minimum wage.
3. Seek alternative ways of providing the benefits that workers who do not have long-term employment contracts with one firm will need, particularly health insurance.
4. Keep some limited demand-side strategies under ongoing consideration, particularly in times of slack labor market demand.

These strategies are not costless. But neither are the social and economic problems that have resulted from the growing gap between top and bottom earners in this country.

Notes

Chapter 1

This work was supported by a generous grant from the John D. and Catherine T. MacArthur Foundation. This chapter benefited from the extremely able research assistance of Andrew Clark West. I also received helpful comments from my assistant Pam Metz. This chapter owes a particular debt to five works, not given justice with footnotes, that contributed greatly to my understanding of these issues: Abraham, Spletzer, and Stewart (1997), Gordon (1995), Kosters (1997), Levy (1996), and Mishel, Bernstein, and Schmitt (1997).

1. Throughout this chapter I use personal consumption expenditure minus 0.5 percent annually to adjust for inflation.
2. Some 38 percent of all persons were children in the 1960s. By the 1980s, the figure had fallen to 27 percent. As a result, even if national income per adult had not changed, national income per person would have risen nearly 18 percent.
3. I first heard this thought experiment used by Robert Reich.
4. Bureau of Economic Analysis price indexes suggest that health prices grew 50 percent in real terms (using the PCE for inflation adjustment) between 1973 and 1996.
5. The maximum earnings for social security and medicare in 1973 was $31,800 (using PCE less 0.5 percent), and the tax rate was 5.85 percent. By 1996 the maximum for social security was $62,700, and there was no limit for medicare. The combined rate was 7.65 percent.
6. Benefits were imputed as follows from data of the Bureau of Economic Analysis. The employer's portion of medicare payroll taxes was imputed based on the statutory tax rate and maximum earnings. Social security and other social insurance costs (such as unemployment insurance) were imputed by taking reported contributions to social insurance less aggregate imputed medicare taxes and apportioning the remainder in proportion to the social security earnings for each worker (that is, earnings up to the social security maximum). Aggregate health insurance and workers compensation benefits were allocated in proportion to individual earnings

below $75,000 if the worker reported having health insurance coverage. Pension costs were apportioned by individual earnings (with no cap). It was assumed that the same proportion of workers in each income tertile had coverage in 1973 as they did in 1980. This assumption is problematic only if the relative change in benefits varied by income class between 1973 and 1980.

7. A better test might be profits relative to total private compensation. That figure looks at virtually identical trends that reached a peak of 26 percent in the 1960s, fell below 15 percent during much of the 1970s, and rose back to 20 percent by 1996.

8. The preferred explanation for the apparent divergence is that it is real, but it does not indicate that capital gained relative to labor because the new higher output per worker was sold at lower real prices. Workers were producing more products that sold for somewhat less. Thus profits did not rise dramatically. I have real questions about this explanation. First of all, it is an explanation by definition. If measured productivity rises and profits do not, measured prices must diverge. Second, it implies that domestic consumer prices (which I use to adjust for inflation) are rising faster than the prices firms get. This can be true in principle if import prices are rising rapidly and export prices are falling. Still the divergence is too large and the trend too long to be properly accounted for in this way. It can also be caused by overstating the consumer price index relative to the producer price index. There is solid evidence that the CPI is overstated, and perhaps the producer price index has fewer problems. Yet many have argued that economists mismeasure productivity and show growth that is *too low*, which would exacerbate the problem. In my view, the recent divergence between productivity and compensation remains an anomaly that merits close attention if it does not vanish soon.

9. Indeed I would have to use income to impute wage rates for persons not working outside the home.

10. Some low-income families would also qualify for the earned income tax credit, which would increase their income in 1996, although taxes were also higher that year due mainly to payroll taxes. No taxes or tax credits are reflected in this, the standard census measure of family income.

Chapter 2

Pat Carey of the Bureau of Labor Statistics and Tom Smith of the National Opinion Research Center provided special tabulations. Dan Shapiro of the Institute for Research on Higher Education of the University of Pennsylvania provided access to and help with national employer survey data. David Ellwood and Rob Valletta provided useful comments.

1. The term shared capitalism is borrowed from the current National Bureau of Economic Research project in which the authors are involved.

2. The data on displacement rates for all workers are from Farber (2000), and the data on long-tenure workers are from Hipple (1999). Both use data from the displaced worker surveys conducted by the Bureau of Labor Statistics, which provides the only source of good representative data. The first series shows higher displacement rates not only because it includes all workers rather than just long-tenure workers, but also because it represents the risk of displacement over a three-year period, while the second series represents the risk of displacement over a two-year period. The rates through 1991 in the first series are slightly higher than in the second series due to an adjustment by Farber to account for a change in the displacement question between the 1992 and 1994 survey (with the pre-1994 surveys using a five-year retrospective question that leads to an undercount of new displacements in the previous three years).

3. Several studies with consistent findings include Schmidt (1999), Stewart (1998b), and Valletta (1997b, 1997c, 1999). The results of Aaronson and Sullivan (1998, 39) suggest that increases in job anxiety during the 1990s are linked to a 0.3 percentage point decline in wage increases per year.

4. Farber found that, of workers displaced in the previous three years, the reemployment rate at the survey date was nine percentage points lower among women than among men, fifteen percentage points lower among nonwhites than among whites, and sixteen percentage points lower among high school graduates than among college graduates.

5. Some of this effect can be explained by multiple job losses after the initial displacement. Among workers who avoid additional displacements, losses in annual earnings are 8 percent (7 percent for hourly wages) one to five years after displacement and 1 percent (4 percent for hourly wages) six or more years after displacement (Stevens 1997, 184).

6. The displacement rate tied to "position or shift abolished" almost doubled, from 1.4 percent in the period from 1981 to 1983 to 2.4 percent in the period from 1993 to 1995. There was also a strong increase in those reporting other reasons, but much of this appears to be due to changes in survey methodology, which led many who left voluntarily to report being displaced. The numbers for the first series in figure 2.1 reflect discounting to adjust for this (Farber 2000).

7. These numbers were provided by Pat Carey of the Local Area Unemployment Statistic Program of the Bureau of Labor Statistics.

8. See columns four to seven in table 2.1. The time-series data are limited because the reporting program, which started in 1986, did not include all states over the period from 1986 to 1991 and did not include corporate reorganization and financial difficulty as possible reasons during this time. Therefore, comparisons across years are only suggestive of national trends. Corporate reorganizations in the 1986 to 1991 period may have fallen under "other" reasons during this time; it is noteworthy that the 15 percent figure for 1996 and 1997 exceeds the drop in the "other" category from 1986

Notes   127

to 1991, indicating a likely rise in extended mass layoffs due to corporate reorganizations. Financial difficulty would also fall under "other" reasons in 1986 to 1991, which strengthens this conclusion. Prior to 1996 and 1997, though, both of these reasons may also have been distributed among the other reasons given.

9. The ten-point decline in jobs with more than ten years tenure is adjusted to a seven-point decline, and the seven-point decline in jobs with more than twenty years tenure is adjusted to a decline of four and a half points, when controlling for changes in demographic, occupational, and industry composition over this period (Farber 1997c, 33).

10. There were particularly sharp drops in median tenure from 15.3 to 10.1 years among men age fifty-five to sixty-four and from 12.8 to 10.1 years among men age forty-five to fifty-four, while there were only small declines among men younger than thirty-five.

11. Bernhardt et al. (1999); Neumark et al. (1999). Allen, Clark, and Schieber (1998), however, did not find less stability within large corporations, and Stewart (1998a) found it only among male high school dropouts.

12. This is according to employer data from the Bureau of Labor Statistics. Employee-reported data indicate that 0.8 percent of all employment is in temporary help services. The discrepancy is probably mostly due to many temporary help employees giving their current client's industry as their industry of employment, rather than the temporary help service industry itself.

13. Of temporary help service employees (with other full-time worker percentages in parentheses), 60 percent (44 percent) are female, 21 percent (12 percent) are under the age of twenty-five, 20 percent (5 percent) are from poor families, and 81 percent (73 percent) do not have college degrees (Blank 1998).

14. Only 37 to 41 percent of those who say they would prefer a noncontingent arrangement, however, actually searched for a job in the past three months (while 6 percent of noncontingent workers did so). See Polivka (1996, 72).

15. The ranges are due to alternative assumptions about how many would prefer other arrangements.

16. The 1995 estimate of 4.6 to 8.5 percent of the workforce in problem contingent jobs is on the high side of the 1995 estimates presented in table 2.2 for all contingent employment. This is primarily due to Blank's inclusion of involuntary part-timers and independent contractors who would prefer traditional arrangements, many of whom are not counted in the Bureau of Labor Statistics estimates in table 2.2.

17. The earnings numbers are based on average weekly earnings for full-time, year-round workers ages twenty-five to thirty-four from the March current population survey. The premium for young women increased from 29 to 56 percent over this time. See Card (1998) for a review of evidence on the causal relation between education and earnings.

18. For example, 56 percent of employers in the 1994 national employer survey reported that the skills required to perform production or support jobs had increased in the past three years, while only 5 percent reported a decrease in required skills. Machin and van Reenen (1998) find that technology has played a major role in changing the structure of skills across major industrial countries.

19. Also employees who receive tuition reimbursements and other educational and training opportunities are less likely to be laid off (Kruse 1998).

20. Constantine and Neumark (1996) find, however, that shifts in the incidence of and returns to training played only a minor role in the widening inequality.

21. Employees were asked whether job loss or layoff in the next twelve months was very likely, fairly likely, not too likely, or not at all likely. The percentage saying "not at all likely" declined from about 65 percent in 1977 to 60 percent in 1982, increased thereafter, but was back down to 60 percent in 1996 (Aaronson and Sullivan 1998, 30).

22. The question asked: "About how easy would it be for you to find a job with another employer with approximately the same income and fringe benefits you now have? Would you say very easy, somewhat easy, or not easy at all?" The percentage saying "not easy at all" increased from 43 percent in 1977 to 52 percent in the 1983 recession but declined to 40 percent by 1996.

23. GSS tabulations reported here were provided by Tom Smith of the National Opinion Research Center.

24. Although gender differences in trends in pay (Ellwood this volume) and long-term employment relationships would lead one to expect gender differences in job satisfaction trends, there is no significant difference between the trends for male and female workers.

25. From CBS and *New York Times* polls in June and December 1995. These and other polling results cited in this section are summarized in documents available from the authors.

26. In the 1996 GSS, 69 percent of workers responded that they would do so, very close to the 70 percent figure when the series began in 1973.

27. The percentage saying that hard work is more important than lucky breaks or help from other people rose from 63 percent across the 1970s to 68 percent in the mid-1990s.

28. The percentage agreeing or strongly agreeing that they have a strong sense of loyalty to their supervisors rose from 62 percent in 1982 (Yankelovich, Skelly, and White poll) to 71 percent in 1992 (Cambridge Reports poll). The percentage saying that they have a lot of trust that their employer will keep its promises was 43 percent in 1989 and 45 percent in 1997 (both from Yankelovich polls).

29. In a special GSS supplement in 1991, between 30 and 40 percent of employees in 1991 strongly agreed, and about 10 percent disagreed, that their per-

sonal performance is important to their employer's success, they are proud to be working for their employer, and they are willing to work harder than they have to for the employer to succeed. Just over one-third said that they would turn down a better-paying job with another employer and that they would take almost any job to keep working for their employer, while less than one-fifth said that they have little loyalty to their employer. The full set of questions and results are as follows (strongly agree, agree, disagree, and strongly disagree): The success of my organization depends a lot on how well I do my job: 38.5, 49.0, 11.2, and 1.3 percent; I am willing to work harder than I have to in order to help this organization succeed: 37.9, 52.0, 9.4, and 0.7 percent; I am proud to be working for this organization: 29.9, 59.4, 9.2, and 1.5 percent; I find that my values and the organization's values are very similar: 20.3, 56.3, 19.5, and 3.9 percent; I feel very little loyalty to this organization: 5.2, 13.0, 44.9, and 37.0 percent; I would turn down another job for more pay in order to stay with this organization: 12.8, 25.3, 44.3, and 17.6 percent; I would take almost any job to keep working for this organization: 10.5, 26.0, 48.0, and 15.6 percent.

30. From a *Money* magazine poll in February 1996.

31. From a Princeton Survey Associates poll in June 1997.

32. From a June 1997 Princeton Survey Associates poll and an April 1995 Yankelovich poll.

33. The first result is from a poll conducted for the Dunlop Commission (Freeman and Rogers 1999), and the second is from a Roper/Virginia Slims poll in November 1994.

34. All polls were conducted between 1994 and 1997. Results are summarized in a document available from the authors.

35. From Gallup polls for the Employee Benefit Research Institute, September 1989 and December 1993, summarized in Kruse and Blasi (1999).

36. This stated opinion may not be a good guide to actual behavior. Employee-owners have sided with managers against hostile raiders in several cases, but there have been too few cases to draw firm conclusions about employee-owners' incentives in these situations.

37. All results in this paragraph are from the Gallup polls for the Employee Benefit Research Institute, September 1989 and December 1993, summarized in Kruse and Blasi (1999).

38. Reviewing research on employee involvement, Levine and Tyson (1990) find that, although purely advisory arrangements (for example, quality circles) generally do not lead to lasting improvements in performance, more substantive arrangements (for example, self-managed teams) generally do, particularly when linked to other changes in organization. In a study of thirty steel-finishing lines, Ichniowski, Shaw, and Prennushi (1997) find that individual practices have little effect but that the combination of work teams, employment security, training, and incentives is linked to higher productivity. In an international study of ninety automobile assembly

plants, MacDuffie (1995) finds that employee involvement and human resource indexes are positively tied to physical productivity and quality measures, particularly where more modern technology is used. Studying thirty-five apparel firms, Dunlop and Weil (1996) find higher profitability where team-oriented work practices are combined with new distribution methods. Based on surveys of public companies, Huselid (1995) finds that indexes of reinforcing human resource practices are linked to better company financial performance, a finding that is reinforced by alternative techniques and more recent data (Huselid and Becker 1996; Huselid, Jackson, and Schuler 1997). Kalleberg and Moody (1994) find positive performance effects of human resource policies in a broadly representative data set of organizations. Employee performance, commitment, and citizenship behavior are enhanced by employee involvement and other human resource practices, according to studies by Tsui et al. (1997), Freeman, Kleiner, and Ostroff (1997), and Cappelli and Rogovsky (1998). Positive effects are found in union as well as nonunion firms (Cooke 1994; Eaton and Voos 1994; Black and Lynch 1997). Case studies of innovative work practices have found similarly positive results (reviewed in Ichniowski et al. 1996). A 1993 meta-analysis of thirty-three studies finds that more than three-fourths of changes in measured outcomes are positive, with stronger results where there are more sweeping changes in organizational policies and practices (Ichniowski et al. 1996, 318).

39. For other reviews reaching similar conclusions, see Kling (1995) and Appelbaum and Batt (1994).

40. Only 15 percent of companies in 1993 had more than 40 percent of employees covered by quality circles, 18 percent had such coverage for job enrichment or redesign, only 5 percent had such coverage for self-managed work teams. Only 12 percent of companies had more than one-third of employees heavily involved in decisions at the job level, while 6 percent also had more than one-third of employees heavily involved in higher-level decisions (Lawler, Mohrman, and Ledford 1995, 35).

41. Core production employees were defined as the largest group of nonsupervisory workers directly involved in the production of the good or service.

42. The representativeness of these data is enhanced by the Census Bureau's access to all establishments and the high survey response rate of 72 percent. There are 3,167 establishments represented in the 1994 data set and 3,081 in the 1997 data set. Although large establishments were oversampled in the NES, the numbers reported here have been weighted to reflect the population of all establishments. The calculations are based on NES data sets obtained from the Institute on Research in Higher Education at the University of Pennsylvania. See Cappelli and Neumark (1999) for additional analysis of these data. We are grateful to Dan Shapiro for help in accessing the data.

43. In addition to the pension, health insurance, and child care benefits shown in table 2.8, other benefits on the NES include severance pay, dental bene-

Notes   131

fits, life insurance, sick pay, paid vacation, and family leave. Only family leave increased, no doubt due to new coverage by the Family and Medical Leave Act of 1993.

44. As noted in table 2.10, firms are awarded points for several practices based on comparisons to similar firms. For the measure of flatness of organization, firms are compared to others in their employment size class, while for mean compensation levels, firms are compared to others in their industry (using residuals from pay regressions for each employee category). To provide a better measure of a high level of resources being spent for each opening, the recruitment and selection measure has been adjusted for turnover (by using the residual from a regression of recruitment and selection costs in the past year on the percentage of employees with less than one year's tenure).

45. Measurement of prevalence may be tainted by sampling error, omission of questions on important practices in high-performance workplaces, or other sources of error. Concerning the outcomes research, results may be skewed by selection bias in the types of firms supplying research data or in the types of firms adopting these practices, which many researchers have tried to take into account (Ichniowski et al. 1996).

46. These and the other figures in this paragraph are based on calculations from the Pension and Welfare Benefits Administration's Form 5500 data for fiscal year 1994. Under ERISA, all pension plan administrators must file Form 5500 on a regular schedule. The employer stock figures reported here are based only on plans with more than 100 participants, since small plans (representing about one-fourth of all defined-contribution pension assets) are not required to report employer stock.

47. In a December 1993 Gallup survey, 21 percent of adults reported owning stock of their employer, while a January 1997 survey by Princeton Survey Research Associates found that 20 percent of adults reported that their or their spouse's employer offers a company stock plan. Also, a March 1996 Gallup poll in central Ohio found that 25 percent of adults reported owning stock in the company for which they work.

48. The first figure is from an ABC News/*Washington Post* poll, October 9, 1997, and the second is from New York Stock Exchange (1990).

49. Estimate made by Corey Rosen of the National Center for Employee Ownership, Oakland, Calif.

50. The behaviors studied include turnover, absenteeism, grievances, tardiness, and injuries.

51. The only finding of lower satisfaction among employee-owners (relative to a national sample) occurred in one of the early ESOPs where the unionized employees had lost a bitter strike the year before (where reminders by management that the strike would hurt ESOP account values brought the response, "We don't vote; we don't control the company; we don't care") (Kruse 1984).

52. Gates (1998) presents a case that increased employee ownership strongly enhances workers' well-being along with business and public interests.

132 Notes

53. From the U.S. Chamber of Commerce survey of employee benefits, 21 percent of firms have profit-sharing plans (U.S. Chamber of Commerce 1997). According to the most recent Bureau of Labor Statistics surveys of employee benefits in medium and large firms, 13 percent of workers are in deferred profit-sharing plans, 4 percent are in cash plans, and about 4 percent have profit-linked employer contributions to savings and thrift plans (Bureau of Labor Statistics 1994, 1997c). The prevalence is slightly lower, totaling 15 to 16 percent, in small private firms. Similar prevalence is reported by young workers (Kruse 1998) and by other sources summarized in Kruse (1993).

54. In addition, employers with profit sharing (not surprisingly) strongly tend to view it favorably and as a factor in firm performance (Kruse 1993, 51–52).

55. This includes only econometric studies with objective productivity measures. Studies using employer opinions of performance, or simple comparisons, also support positive effects of profit sharing (Kruse 1993, 52–53).

56. As an illustration of mixed findings, Kruse (1993) finds no general stabilizing effect of all types of profit sharing but does find smaller employment decreases in response to downturns when the profit share appeared to substitute for fixed compensation in rewarding worker effort (which is assumed by the theory). The most recent study follows a large representative sample of young workers over a six-year period and finds that those with profit sharing are less likely to be laid off (controlling for a variety of personal, job, and company characteristics; Kruse 1998).

57. Scanlon, Rucker, and ImproShare plans establish a productivity measure for a base period (based on a ratio of labor costs or hours to output) and then share cost savings with workers if productivity improves over that base period. For productivity measures the Scanlon plan uses labor costs divided by the total value of output, the Rucker plan uses labor costs divided by the value added in production, and the ImproShare plan uses work hours to produce a given amount of output (so that, unlike the Scanlon and Rucker plans, the measure is not affected by product demand or price). The Scanlon and Rucker plans emphasize employee involvement to generate cost-saving ideas.

58. Summarized in Collins (1998). In addition, a large-scale effort to identify "organizational performance-based reward plans" found 2,200 formula-based plans covering more than twenty employees with a cash component, from which a sample indicated that 57 percent (about 1,250 of the total) could be classified as gain-sharing plans based on operational goals (McAdams and Hawk 1992). The project began with 10,000 plans identified through a variety of methods.

59. Independent raters found improvements of organizational effectiveness in 80 percent of cases, employee attitudes in 72 percent, innovation in 89 percent, labor-management cooperation in 67 percent, and pay and rewards in 91 percent of cases.

60. These paths were outlined by Alan Blinder of Princeton University, former vice chair of the Federal Reserve Board and member of President Clinton's Council of Economic Advisers, in his speech at the National Bureau of Economic Research conference on Shared Capitalism, Washington, D.C., May 23, 1998.

References

Aaronson, Daniel, and Daniel G. Sullivan. 1998. "The Decline of Job Security in the 1990s: Displacement, Anxiety, and Their Effect on Wage Growth." *Economic Perspectives*, Federal Reserve Bank of Chicago (first quarter): 17–43.

Abraham, Katherine G., James R. Spletzer, and Jay C. Stewart. 1997. "Divergent Trends in Alternative Wage Series." Unpublished paper. Washington: Bureau of Labor Statistics (August).

Addison, John T., Douglas A. Fox, and Christopher J. Ruhm. 1995. "Trade and Displacement in Manufacturing." *Monthly Labor Review* 118(April): 58–67.

Advisory Commission to Study the Consumer Price Index, Michael J. Boskin, chairman. 1996. "Toward a More Accurate Measure of the Cost of Living." Final Report to the Senate Finance Committee (December).

Allen, Steven G., Robert L. Clark, and Sylvester J. Schieber. 1998. "Has Job Security Vanished in Large Corporations?" Unpublished paper. Raleigh: North Carolina State University, Department of Economics (May).

American Capital Strategies. 1998. "Employee-Owned Companies Continue to Significantly Outperform the Market for the Fifth Consecutive Year." Bethesda, Md.: American Capital Strategies (April 15 press release).

Appelbaum, Eileen, and Rosemary Batt. 1994. *The New American Workplace: Transforming Work Systems in the United States*. Ithaca, N.Y.: ILR Press.

Arthur, Michael B., and Denise M. Rousseau, eds. 1996. *The Boundaryless Career: A New Employment Principle for a New Organizational Era*. New York: Oxford University Press.

Baker, Dean. 1997. "Appendix C: The Measurement of Inflation." In *The State of Working America*, by Lawrence Mishel, Jared Bernstein, and John Schmitt. Armonk, N.Y.: M.E. Sharp.

Barker, Kathleen, and Kathleen Christensen, eds. 1998. *Contingent Work: American Employment Relations in Transition*. Ithaca, N.Y.: Cornell University Press.

Bell, Linda, and Douglas Kruse. 1995. "ESOPs, Profit Sharing, and Gain Sharing in Airlines and High-Technology Industries." Report to the U.S. Department of Labor. Washington, D.C. (March).

Bernhardt, Annette, Martina Morris, Mark Handcock, and Marc Scott. 1999. "Trends in Job Instability and Wages for Young Adult Men." *Journal of Labor Economics* 17(October): S65–90.

Black, Sandra E., and Lisa M. Lynch. 1997. "How to Compete: The Impact of Workplace Practices and Information Technology on Productivity." NBER Working paper 6120. Cambridge, Mass.: National Bureau of Economic Research.

Blair, Margaret, Douglas Kruse, and Joseph Blasi. 2000. "Is Employee Ownership an Unstable Form? Or a Stabilizing Force?" In *The New Relationship: Human Capital in the American Corporation*, edited by Margaret Blair and Thomas Kochan. Washington, D.C.: Brookings Institution.

Blank, Rebecca. 1998. "Contingent Work in a Changing Labor Market." In *Generating Jobs: How to Increase Demand for Less-Skilled Workers*, edited by Richard Freeman and Peter Gottschalk. New York: Russell Sage Foundation.

Blasi, Joseph, Michael Conte, and Douglas Kruse. 1996. "Employee Stock Ownership and Corporate Performance among Public Companies." *Industrial and Labor Relations Review* 50(October): 60–79.

Blasi, Joseph, and Douglas Kruse. 1991. *The New Owners: The Mass Emergence of Employee Ownership in Public Companies and What It Means to American Business*. New York: HarperCollins.

Blau, Francine. 1998. "Trends in the Well-Being of American Women, 1970–1995." *Journal of Economic Literature* 36 (March): 112–65.

Blau, Francine D., and Lawrence M. Kahn. 1996. *Wage Inequality: International Comparisons and Its Sources*. Washington, D.C.: AEI Press.

Bollier, David. 1998. "Work and Future Society: Where Are the Economy and Technology Taking Us?" Report prepared for the Aspen Institute Domestic Strategy Group. Washington, D.C.: Aspen Institute.

Bonin, John, Derek Jones, and Louis Putterman. 1993. "Theoretical and Empirical Studies of Producer Cooperatives: Will Ever the Twain Meet?" *Journal of Economic Literature* 31(September): 1290–1320.

Bowers, Norman, and Paul Swaim. 1994. "Recent Trends in Job Training." *Contemporary Economic Policy* 12(January): 79–88.

Brickley, J. A., and K. T. Hevert. 1991. "Direct Employee Stock Ownership: An Empirical Investigation." *Financial Management* 20(Summer): 70–84.

Bullock, R. J., and M. E. Tubbs. 1990. "A Case Meta-Analysis of Gain Sharing Plans as Organizational Development Mechanisms." *Journal of Applied Behavioral Science* 26(3): 383–404.

Cappelli, Peter. 1993. "Are Skill Requirements Rising? Evidence from Production and Clerical Jobs." *Industrial and Labor Relations Review* 46(April): 515–30.

Cappelli, Peter, Laurie Bassi, Harry Katz, David Knoke, Paul Osterman, and Michael Useem. 1997. *Change at Work*. New York: Oxford University Press.

Cappelli, Peter, and David Neumark. 1999. "Do 'High-Performance' Work Practices Improve Establishment-Level Outcomes?" NBER Working Paper 7374. Cambridge, Mass.: National Bureau of Economic Research (October).

Cappelli, Peter, and Nikolai Rogovsky. 1998. "Employee Involvement and Organizational Citizenship: Implications for Labor Law and 'Lean Production.'" *Industrial and Labor Relations Review* 51(July): 633–53.

Card, David. 1998. "The Causal Effect of Education on Earnings." Working Paper 2. Berkeley: University of California, Berkeley, Center for Labor Economics.

Cascio, Wayne F. 1993. "Downsizing: What Do We Know? What Have We Learned?" *Academy of Management Executive* 7(1): 95–104.

Chubb, John E., and Terry M. Moe. 1990. *Politics, Markets, and America's Schools.* Washington, D.C.: Brookings Institution Press.

Cohany, Sharon. 1998. "Workers in Alternative Employment Arrangements: A Second Look." *Monthly Labor Review* 121(11): 3–21.

Coleman, James S., Thomas Hoffer, and Sally Kilgore. 1982. *High School Achievement: Public, Catholic, and Private Schools Compared.* New York: Basic Books.

Collins, Denis. 1998. *Gain Sharing and Power: Lessons from Six Scanlon Plans.* Ithaca, N.Y.: Cornell University Press.

Commission on the Future of Worker Management Relations. 1994. "Fact Finding Report." Washington: Department of Commerce and Department of Labor.

Commission on the Skills of the American Workforce. 1990. *America's Choice: High Skills or Low Wages.* Washington: National Center on the Educational Quality of the Workforce.

Committee for Economic Development. 1998. *The Employer's Role in Linking School and Work.* New York and Washington, D.C.: Committee for Economic Development.

Constantine, Jill, and David Neumark. 1996. "Training and the Growth of Wage Inequality." *Industrial Relations* 35(October): 491–510.

Cooke, William N. 1994. "Employee Participation, Group-Based Pay Incentives, and Firm Performance: A Union-Nonunion Comparison." *Industrial and Labor Relations Review* 47(July): 594–609.

Council of Economic Advisers. 1998. *Economic Report of the President.* Washington: U.S. Government Printing Office.

Dunlop, John T., and David Weil. 1996a. "Diffusion and Performance of Modular Production in the U.S. Apparel Industry." *Industrial Relations* 35(July): 334–55.

Eaton, Adrienne E., and Paula B. Voos. 1994b. "Productivity-Enhancing Innovations in Work Organization, Compensation, and Employee Participation in the Union versus the Nonunion Sectors." In *Advances in Industrial and Labor Relations,* edited by David Lewin and Donna Sockell. Vol. 6. Greenwich and London: JAI Press.

Ellwood, David T., and Thomas Kane. 2000. "Who Is Getting a College Education? Family Background and the Growing Gaps in Enrollment." In *Securing the Future: Investing in Children from Birth to College,* edited by Jane Waldfogel and Sheldon Danziger. New York: Russell Sage.

Fairlie, Robert W., and Lori G. Kletzer. 1996. "Race and the Shifting Burden of Job Displacement: 1982–93." *Monthly Labor Review* 119(September): 13–23.

Farber, Henry S. 1997a. "The Changing Face of Job Loss in the United States 1981–1995." Working paper 382. Princeton, N.J.: Princeton University, Industrial Relations Section.

———. 1997b. "The Changing Face of Job Loss in the United States 1981–1995." *Brookings Papers on Economic Activity: Microeconomics,* 55–128.

———. 1997c. "Trends in Long-Term Employment in the United States 1979–96." Working paper 384. Princeton, N.J.: Princeton University, Industrial Relations Section.

———. 1998. "Has the Rate of Job Loss Increased in the Nineties?" Working paper 394. Princeton, N.J.: Princeton University, Industrial Relations Section.

———. 2000. "Job Loss and Long-Term Employment in the U.S.: 1981–1997." Working paper. Princeton, N.J.: Princeton University, Industrial Relations Section.

Fortin, Nicole, M., and Thomas Lemieux. 1997. "Institutional Charges and Rising Wage Inequality: Is There a Linkage?" *Journal of Economic Perspectives* 9(3): 15–33.

Frazis, Harley, Maury Gittleman, Michael Horrigan, and Mary Joyce. 1998. "Results from the 1995 Survey of Employer-Provided Training." *Monthly Labor Review* 121(June): 3–13.

Freeman, Richard B. 1995. "Are Your Wages Set in Beijing?" *Journal of Economic Perspectives* 9(3): 15–33.

———. 1997. *When Earnings Diverge: Causes, Consequences, and Cures for the New Inequality in the U.S.* Report 284. Washington D.C.: National Policy Association.

Freeman, Richard, Morris Kleiner, and Cheri Ostroff. 1997. "The Anatomy and Effects of Employee Involvement." Unpublished paper. Cambridge, Mass./Minneapolis, Minn.: Harvard University and University of Minnesota (July).

Freeman, Richard, and Joel Rogers. 1999. *What Workers Want.* Ithaca, New York/New York: Cornell University Press/Russell Sage.

Friedlander, Daniel, David H. Greenberg, and Philip K. Robins. 1997. "Evaluating Government Training Programs for the Economically Disadvantaged." *Journal of Economic Literature* 34(4): 1809–55.

Gates, Jeff. 1998. *The Ownership Solution: Toward a Shared Capitalism for the Twenty-first Century.* Reading, Mass.: Addison-Wesley.

General Accounting Office. 1986. *Employee Stock Ownership Plans: Benefits and Costs of ESOP Tax Incentives for Broadening Stock Ownership.* GAO/PEMD-87-8. Washington: General Accounting Office.

Gittleman, Maury, Michael Horrigan, and Mary Joyce. 1998. "'Flexible' Workplace Practices: Evidence from a Nationally Representative Survey." *Industrial and Labor Relations Review* 52(October): 99–115.

Gordon, Robert J. 1995. "The American Real Wage since 1963: Is It Unchanged or Has It More Than Doubled?" Unpublished paper. Evanston, Ill.: Northwestern University (December 1995).

Greenwood, Jeremy. 1997. *The Third Industrial Revolution: Technology, Productivity, and Income Inequality.* Washington, D.C.: AEI Press.

Hansen, Daniel G. 1997. "Worker Performance and Group Incentives: A Case Study." *Industrial and Labor Relations Review* 51(October): 37–49.

Haveman. Robert. 1994. "The Influence of Changing trade Patterns on Displacement of Labor." Unpublished paper. Purdue University, Krannert School of Management.

Hipple, Steven. 1998. "Contingent Work: Results from the Second Survey." *Monthly Labor Review* 121(November): 22–35.

———. 1999. "Worker Displacement in the Mid-1990s." *Monthly Labor Review* 122(July): 15–32.

Hipple, Steven, and Jay Stewart. 1996. "Earnings and Benefits of Contingent and Noncontingent Workers." *Monthly Labor Review* 119(October): 46–54.

Hoxby, Caroline M. 1998. "The Economics of School Reform." *NBER Reporter* (Spring): 6–12.

Huselid, Mark. 1995. "The Impact of Human Resource Management Practices on Turnover, Productivity, and Corporate Financial Performance." *Academy of Management Journal* 38(3): 635–72.

Huselid, Mark, and Brian Becker. 1996. "Methodological Issues in Cross-Sectional and Panel Estimates of the HR-Firm Performance Link." *Industrial Relations* 35(3): 400–22.

Huselid, Mark, Susan Jackson, and Randall Schuler. 1997. "Technical and Strategic Human Resource Management Effectiveness as Determinants of Firm Performance." *Academy of Management Journal* 40(1): 171–88.

Ichniowski, Casey, Thomas A. Kochan, David Levine, Craig Olson, and George Strauss. 1996. "What Works at Work: Overview and Assessment." *Industrial Relations* 35(July): 299–333.

Ichniowski, Casey, Kathryn Shaw, and Giovanna Prennushi. 1997. "The Impact of Human Resource Management Practices on Productivity." *American Economic Review* 87(June): 291–313.

Jackson, Susan, and Randall Schuler. 1995. "Understanding Human Resource Management in the Context of Organizations and Their Environments." *Annual Review of Psychology* 46: 237–64.

Jacobson, Louis S., Robert J. LaLonde, and Daniel G. Sullivan. 1993. "Earnings Losses of Displaced Workers." *American Economic Review* 83(September): 685–709.

Johnson, George E. 1997. "Changes in Earnings Inequality: The Role of Demand Shifts." *Journal of Economic Perspectives* 11(2): 41–54.

Jones, Derek. 1979. "U.S. Producer Cooperatives: The Record to Date." *Industrial Relations* 18(3): 343–56.

Kalleberg, Arne L., and Peter V. Marsden. 1995. "Organizational Commitment and Job Performance in the U.S. Labor Force." *Research in the Sociology of Work* 5: 235–57.

Kalleberg, Arne L., and James W. Moody. 1994. "Human Resource Management and Organizational Performance." *American Behavioral Scientist* 37(June): 948–62.

Kardas, Peter, Adria L. Scharf, and Jim Keogh. 1998. "Wealth and Income Consequences of Employee Ownership: A Comparative Study from Washington State." Unpublished paper. Olympia: Washington State Department of Community, Trade, and Economic Development.

Kaufman, Roger T. 1992. "The Effects of ImproShare on Productivity." *Industrial and Labor Relations Review* 45(January): 311–22.

Kim, Dong-One. 1996. "Factors Influencing Organizational Performance in Gain Sharing Programs." *Industrial Relations* 35(April): 227–44.

Kletzer, Lori G. 1998. "Job Displacement." *Journal of Economic Perspectives* 12(1): 115–36.

Kling, Jeffrey. 1995. "High-Performance Work Systems and Firm Performance." *Monthly Labor Review* 118(May): 29–36.

Kosters, Marvin. 1997. "Wage Levels and Inequality: Interpreting the Trends." Paper prepared for the American Enterprise Institute, Seminar on Understanding Economic Inequality. Washington, D.C. (October 1997).

Krueger, Alan. 1993. "How Computers Have Changed the Wage Structure: Evidence from Microdata, 1984–89." *Quarterly Journal of Economics* 108(1): 33–60.

Krueger, Alan, and Aaron Siskind. 1997. "Assessing Bias in the Consumer Price Index from Survey Data." Working paper 392. Princeton, N.J.: Industrial Relations Section, Princeton University.

Kruse, Douglas. 1984. *Employee Ownership and Employee Attitudes: Two Case Studies*. Norwood, Penn.: Norwood Editions.

———. 1993. *Profit Sharing: Does It Make a Difference?* Kalamazoo, Mich.: W. E. Upjohn Institute for Employment Research.

———. 1996. "Why Do Firms Adopt Profit Sharing and Employee Ownership Plans?" *British Journal of Industrial Relations* 34(December): 515–38.

———. 1998. "Profit Sharing and the Demand for Low-Skill Workers." In *Generating Jobs: Increasing the Demand for Low-Skill Workers*, edited by Richard Freeman and Peter Gottschalk. New York: Russell Sage Foundation.

Kruse, Douglas, and Joseph Blasi. 1997. "Employee Ownership, Employee Attitudes, and Firm Performance: A Review of the Evidence." In *Handbook of Human Resource Management*, edited by Daniel J. B. Mitchell, David Lewin, and Mahmood Zaidi. Greenwich, Conn.: JAI Press.

———. 1999. "Public Opinion Polls on Employee Ownership and Profit Sharing." *Journal of Employee Ownership Law and Finance* 11(3): 3–25.

Lawler, Edward E., Susan A. Mohrman, and Gerald E. Ledford. 1995. *Creating High-Performance Organizations*. San Francisco: Jossey-Bass.

Lerman, Robert I. 1997. *Meritocracy without Rising Inequality?* Washington, D.C.: Urban Institue Press.

Levine, David I. 1992. "Public Policy Implications of Imperfections in the Market for Worker Participation." *Economic and Industrial Democracy* 13(May): 183–206.

———. 1995. *Reinventing the Workplace: How Business and Employees Can Both Win*. Washington, D.C.: Brookings Institution Press.

Levine, David I., and Laura D'Andrea Tyson. 1990. "Participation, Productivity, and the Firm's Environment." In *Paying for Productivity: A Look at the Evidence*, edited by Alan Blinder, 183–236. Washington, D.C.: Brookings Institution Press.

Levy, Frank. 1996. "Where Did the Money Go? A Layman's Guide to Recent Trends in U.S. Living Standards." MIT Industrial Performance Center working paper 96–008. Cambridge, Mass.: Massachusetts Institute of Technology.

Lillard, Lee, and Hong Tan. 1992. "Private Sector Training: Who Gets It and What Are Its Effects?" *Research in Labor Economics* 13: 1–62.

Lynch, Lisa. 1992. "Private-Sector Training and the Earnings of Young Workers." *American Economic Review* 11(1): 299–312.

———. 1994. "Payoffs to Alternative Training Strategies at Work." In *Working under Different Rules*, edited by Richard Freeman, 63–96. New York: Russell Sage Foundation.

MacDuffie, John Paul. 1995. "Human Resource Bundles and Manufacturing Performance: Organizational Logic and Flexible Production Systems in the World Auto Industry." *Industrial and Labor Relations Review* 48(January): 197–221.

Machin, Stephen, and John van Reenen. 1998. "Technology and Changes in Skill Structure: Evidence from Seven OECD Countries." Working Paper 3. Berkeley: Center for Labor Economics, University of California, Berkeley (May).

McAdams, Jerry L., and Elizabeth J. Hawk. 1992. *Capitalizing on Human Assets.* Scottsdale, Ariz.: American Compensation Association.

Mishel, Lawrence, Jared Bernstein, and John Schmitt. 1997. *The State of Working America.* Armonk, N.Y.: M. E. Sharp.

Mitchell, Daniel J. B. 1995. "Profit Sharing and Employee Ownership: Policy Implications." *Contemporary Economic Policy* 13(April): 16–25.

Nardone, Thomas, Jonathan Veum, and Julie Yates. 1997. "Measuring Job Security." *Monthly Labor Review* 120(June): 26–33.

National Center for Employee Ownership. 1999. *The Stock Options Book.* Oakland, Calif.: National Center for Employee Ownership.

National Commission on Excellence in Education. 1983. *A Nation at Risk.* Washington, D.C.: National Commission on Excellence in Education.

Neumark, David, Daniel Polsky, and Daniel Hansen. 1999. "Has Job Stability Declined Yet? New Evidence for the 1990s." *Journal of Labor Economics* 17(October): S29–64.

New York Stock Exchange. 1990. *Share Ownership 1990.* New York: New York Stock Exchange.

Office of Technology Assessment. 1995. *Learning to Work.* Washington, D.C.: U.S. Congress.

Osterman, Paul. 1994. "How Common Is Workplace Transformation and Who Adopts It?" *Industrial and Labor Relations Review* 47(January): 173–88.

———. 2000. "Work Reorganization in an Era of Restructuring." *Industrial and Labor Relations Review* 53(2): 179–96.

Peterson, Paul E., and Bryan Hassel. 1998. *Learning from School Choice.* Washington, D.C.: Brookings Institution Press.

Polivka, Anne E. 1996. "Into Contingent and Alternative Employment: By Choice?" *Monthly Labor Review* 119 (October): 55–74.

Poterba, James M., and Andrew A. Samwick. 1995. "Stock Ownership Patterns, Stock Market Fluctuations, and Consumption." *Brookings Papers on Economic Activity* 2. Washington, D.C.: Brookings.

Schmidt, Stephanie R. 1999b. "Long-Run Trends in Workers' Beliefs about Their Own Job Security: Evidence from the General Social Survey." *Journal of Labor Economics* 17(October): S127–41.

Schuster, Michael. 1983. "The Impact of Union-Management Cooperation on Productivity and Employment." *Industrial and Labor Relations Review* 36(April): 425–30.

———. 1984. "The Scanlon Plan: A Longitudinal Analysis." *Journal of Applied Behavioral Science* 36(April): 23–38.

Schwartz, Peter, and Peter Leyden. 1977. "The Long Boom." *Wired* (July): 115–73.

Smith, Nelson. 1996b. *Standards Mean Business.* Washington, D.C.: National Alliance of Business.

Stevens, Ann Huff. 1997. "Persistent Effects of Job Displacement: The Importance of Multiple Job Losses." *Journal of Labor Economics* 15(January): 165–88.

Stewart, Jay. 1998a. "Has Job Mobility Increased? Evidence from the Current Population Survey: 1975–1995." Working paper 308. Washington: U.S. Bureau of Labor Statistics (February).

———. 1998b. "Job Security in the 1990s." Working paper 316. Washington: U.S. Bureau of Labor Statistics.

Topel, Robert H. 1997. "Factor Proportions and Relative Wages: The Supply-Side Determinants of Wage Inequality." *Journal of Economic Perspectives* 11(2): 55–74.

Tsui, Anne S., Jone L. Pearce, Lyman W. Porter, and Angela M. Tripoli. 1997. "Alternative Approaches to the Employee-Organization Relationship: Does Investment in Employees Pay Off?" *Academy of Management Journal* 40(5): 1089–121.

U.S. Chamber of Commerce. 1997. *Employee Benefits.* Washington: U.S. Chamber of Commerce.

U.S. Department of Labor. 1994. *Survey of Employee Benefits in Medium and Large Firms.* Washington: Bureau of Labor Statistics.

———. 1995. *What's Working (and What's Not): A Summary of Research on the Economic Impacts of Employment and Training Programs.* Washington: Office of the Chief Economist (January).

———. 1996a. "1995 Survey of Employer-Provided Training—Employer Results." News Release USDL 96-268. Washington: Bureau of Labor Statistics (July 10).

———. 1996b. "1995 Survey of Employer-Provided Training—Employee Results." News Release USDL 96-515. Washington: Bureau of Labor Statistics (December 19).

———. 1997a. "Contingent and Alternative Employment Arrangements, February 1997." News Release USDL 97-422. Washington: Bureau of Labor Statistics (December 2).

———. 1997b. "Job Tenure Summary." News Release USDL 97-25. Washington: Bureau of Labor Statistics (January 30).

———. 1997c. "Survey of Employee Benefits in Medium and Large Firms." Washington: Bureau of Labor Statistics.

———. 1998a. "Abstract of 1994 Form 5500 Annual Reports." *Private Pension Plan Bulletin,* Pension and Welfare Benefits Administration, (Spring).

———. 1998b. "Are Workers More Secure?" Summary 98-5. Washington: U.S. Bureau of Labor Statistics (May).

U.S. Senate. 1939. "Survey of Experiences in Profit Sharing and Possibilities of Incentive Taxation." Subcommittee of the Committee on Finance. Washington: Government Printing Office.

Valletta, Robert G. 1997a. "The Effects of Industry Employment Shifts on the Wage Structure, 1979–1995." *Economic Review,* Federal Reserve Bank of San Francisco, 1: 16–32.

———. 1997b. "Job Loss during the 1990s." Weekly letter 97-95. San Francisco: Federal Reserve Bank of San Francisco (February 21).

———. 1997c. "Job Security Update." Weekly Letter 97-34. San Francisco: Federal Reserve Bank of San Francisco (November 14).

———. 1999. "Declining Job Security." *Journal of Labor Economics* 17(October): S170–97.

Weitzman, Martin. 1984. *The Share Economy.* Cambridge, Mass.: Harvard University Press.

Weitzman, Martin, and Douglas Kruse. 1990. "Profit Sharing and Productivity." In *Paying for Productivity: A Look at the Evidence*, edited by Alan S. Blinder. Washington, D.C.: Brookings Institution.

Welbourne, Theresa M., David B. Balkin, and Luis R. Gómez-Mejía. 1995. "Gain Sharing and Mutual Monitoring: A Combined Agency-Organizational Justice Interpretation." *Academy of Management Journal* 38(June): 881–99.

Wilson, Nicholas, and Michael Peel. 1991. "The Impact on Absenteeism and Quits of Profit-Sharing and Other Forms of Employee Participation." *Industrial and Labor Relations Review* 44(April): 454–68.

Index

Boldface numbers refer to figures and tables.

Aspen Institute, Domestic Strategy Group (DSG), vii–ix, xiii–xiv

Blank, Rebecca, viii, xi–xiii, 55
Blasi, Joseph, viii, x–xi
Blinder, Alan, viii, 1, 133*n*60
Bollier, David, vii
Boskin Commission, 7, 93–94
Buchanan, Pat, 11

capital: components of, **21**; returns to and national income, 20–23
Card, David, 116
child care, 118–19
children: economic fortunes of, x, 28–29; family income, impact of low, 109; family income and structure, **29**, **41**; and interpreting national income distribution, 3; percentage in the population, 124*n*2. *See also* families
civic cohesion, 110
Coleman, James, 98–99
Collins, Denis, 85
Commission on the Skills of the American Workforce, 69

contingent work, 52–55, 86
CPI. *See* current price index
CPS. *See* current population survey
current population survey (CPS), 8–9, 14–16
current price index (CPI), 7

displacement of workers. *See* worker displacement
DSG. *See* Aspen Institute, Domestic Strategy Group

earned income tax credit (EITC), xii, xiv, 101–2, 115–18
economy: condition of American, 92; data sources, 8–9, 32–33; difficulties in understanding, 1–5; distribution of rising incomes (*see* inequality; wages); inflation adjustments, 5–8, 93–94; national income (*see* national income); summary of recent changes, 30–33
education: earnings premium for, 55; families and income growth, 23–28; improvement of, xii, xiv, 98–100, 111–13; and increased wage vari-

143

ance, 95; and reemployment after displacement, 47; studies of, 98–99; vouchers, 99–100, 112–13; and wages of men, 9. *See also* training

EITC. *See* earned income tax credit

Ellwood, David, viii–ix, 29

employees. *See* workers

employee stock ownership plans (ESOPs), xi, 79, 81, 85–87, 132*n*51

employers: attitudes of employees regarding, 63–66; displacement of workers (*see* worker displacement); employees, relationship with, 43, 50–52, 86–91 (*see also* worker displacement; workers); high-performance productivity strategies, x, 66–71, **72–77**, 78, **80**; training and relationships with employees, 55–56, 58, 61–63

employment. *See* employers; work; workers

employment rate: American, 92; U.S. compared to Europe, 97, **98**

ESOPs. *See* employee stock ownership plans

families: and income distribution, x, 23–24; income and family structure, 29–30, 96; income of single-parent, 26–28, **40–41**; income of two-parent, 24–26, **39–40**; of less-skilled workers, 108–9; and the wages of men, 11. *See also* children

Farber, Henry, 50

Freeman, Richard, 95

gain sharing, 84–87

Gallatin, Albert, 82

government: earned income tax credit (EITC), xii, xiv, 99–100, 115–18; European model, 96–98; inequality, role in addressing, xi–xii; support for low-income families, 26. *See also* public policy

Haveman, Robert, 47

health benefits, 13–16, 18, 118–19

Heckman, James, 114

high-performance work practices: adoption and use of, 66–71, 78, **80**, 87; index of, **76–77**; policy recommendations, 89–90; and productivity, x. *See also* workplace

Ichniowski, Casey, 67, 69

immigration, 95, 104, 122–23

income. *See* capital, returns to and national income; national income; wages

inequality: causes of wage, 93–96, 105–6; government role in addressing, xi–xii (*see also* government; public policy); increase in wage, 16, 20, 30–32, 123; reasons to care about wage, 106–11; redistribution, 97; and returns to capital, 22–23; and training, 58. *See also* less-skilled workers; wages

inflation, adjustments for in economic statistics, 5–8, 93–94

international trade, 48, 94–96, 104, 119–20

Jacobson, Louis, 47

Jevons, William Stanley, 82

job stability and security, 50–52 *See also* contingent work; worker displacement

Job Training Partnership Act, 114

Kane, Thomas, 29

Krueger, Alan, 116

Kruse, Douglas, viii, x–xi

labor law, 102–3

labor market: adjustment of, 107–8; European model, 96–97; institutions of and wage variance, 96

labor unions, 96, 120–21

LaLonde, Robert, 47

layoffs. *See* worker displacement

less-skilled workers: families of, 108–9; and labor unions, 120–21; problems confronting, xii–xiii, 97;

productivity and labor market adjustment, 107–8; public policy recommendations for aiding, 101–2; strategies to increase demand for, 119–20; training, 115 (*see also* education; training); and wage variance, 95–96. *See also* inequality
Long, Russell, 79, 89

men: fraction at different wage levels with health and pension benefits, 13; fraction married and living with spouse, **31**; job satisfaction, 128*n*24; less-skilled, problems of, xiii (*see also* less-skilled workers); long-tenure jobs, 50; national income per person and median earnings, **2**; wages of, ix, 2–5, 9–16, **35–37**, 106 (*see also* wages); wage variance by sex, 96
Mill, John Stuart, 82
minimum wage, 115–17

national employer surveys (NES), 69
national income: adjusted for inflation, **34–35**; compared to earnings of full-time male workers, 2–5; per adult and components, **4**; returns to capital and, 20–23; wages (*see* wages)
national income and product accounts (NIPA), 2, 8–9
NES. *See* national employer surveys
Newman, Katherine, xiv
NIPA. *See* national income and product accounts
Niskanen, William, viii, xi–xiii

OECD. *See* Organization for Economic Cooperation and Development
Organization for Economic Cooperation and Development (OECD), wage variance, 95–96
ownership, employee: attitudes and performance, impact on, 65, 80–82, 85–87; employee stock ownership plans (ESOPs), 79, 81, 85–86; non-ESOP plans, 79–80; policy recommendations, 88–90; stock options, 80; worker cooperatives, 80

part-time employment, 53, 55, 70
PCE. *See* personal consumption expenditure index
pension benefits, 13–16, 18, 121–22
personal consumption expenditure index (PCE), 7
productivity: and employee ownership (*see* ownership, employee); and gain sharing, 84–87; growth in related to wages, 23, 32–33; high-performance strategies (*see* high-performance work practices); less-skilled workers and labor market adjustment, 107–8; and profit sharing, xi, 82–87; technology and wage variance, 93–94; and training, x, 55–63, 70–71
profit-sharing, xi, 82–87
public policy: demand-side strategies, 119–20; education (*see* education); effects of changing on single mothers, **117**; employment subsidies, 118–19; European model, 96–97; immigration, 95, 104, 122–23; labor management and unions, 120–22; less-skilled workers, 97, 101–2; minimum wage, 115–17; recommendations, 88–91, 102–4, 123; taxation (*see* tax policy); training (*see* training). *See also* government

quality circles, x, xii, 67–69, **80**, 130*n*40, 102–3

race: and family income, 28; reemployment after displacement, 47; and wage variance, 96
redistribution, 97

self-managed work teams, x, 69–70, **77, 80**, 130*n*40

sex: and wage variance, 96, 106. *See also* men; women
skills. *See* training
Stevens, Ann Huff, 47
stock options, 80
subsidies: employment, 118–19; wage, 115–18
Sullivan, Daniel, 47

tax policy: business tax and high-performance workplace practices, 90–91; earned income tax credit (EITC), xii, xiv, 101–2, 115–18; profit sharing and employee ownership, 90; proposals, 103–4
technology, productivity and wage variance, 93–94
temporary work, 52–56, 70, 120–21
trade, international, 48, 94–95, 104, 119–20
training: employer-provided, 55–63, 70, 78, 86; problems and public policy considerations, 100–1, 113–15

unemployment rate, 92

vouchers, 99–100, 112–13

wages: and the composition of employment, 93, 106; distribution of, ix–x, 30–33 (*see also* inequality); family, 23–30; and immigration, 95; inequality in, reasons to care about, 106–11; and international trade, 94–95; of men (*see* men); minimum, 115–17; ratio of aggregate CPS to NIPA data, **33**; relative to profits, **22**; subsidies, 115–18; technology and productivity, 93–94; of women (*see* women)
Weitzman, Martin, 83

welfare, 26
women: economic fortunes of in the changing economy, ix; effects of changing policy on single mothers, **117**; family structure and earnings, 109; fraction at different wage levels with health and pension benefits, **18**; job satisfaction, 128*n*24; long-tenure jobs, 50; reemployment after displacement, 47; wages of, 4–5, 16–20, **37–39**, 106; wage variance by sex, 96
work: composition of employment, 93; contingent, 52–56; devaluing of, 109–10; efforts of Domestic Strategy Group, vii–ix, xiii–xiv; high-performance productivity strategies (*see* high-performance work practices); "problem" contingent work, prevalence of, **56**; satisfaction with, trends in, **64**
worker cooperatives, 80
worker displacement: costs of, 46–47; rates and trends, x, 43–46, 70, 86; reasons for, 47–50
workers: attitudes, 63–66; displacement (*see* worker displacement); employers, relationship with, 43, 50–52, 86–91 (*see also* employers; ownership, employee); income of full-year, full-time male, 2–5; less-skilled (*see* less-skilled workers); long-term employment, 50–52; participation in ownership (*see* ownership, employee); training, x, 55–63
workplace: characteristics, **72–73**; and gain sharing, 84–85; high-performance work practices (*see* high-performance work practices; organization, **74–75**; and profit sharing, 82–84